# Food-Safe
# Kitchens

# Food-Safe Kitchens

*presenting*

## EIGHT FOOD-SAFE STEPS

## Ann Marchiony

Written expressly for the home cook.

*Food-Safe Kitchens* is edited by a baker's dozen
of professional food safety experts.

"That '24-hour flu?' It might be something you ate!"

Dr. Robert Tauxe

PEARSON

Prentice
Hall

Upper Saddle River
New Jersey, 07458

**Library of Congress Cataloging-in-Publication Data**

Marchiony, Ann.
 Food-safe kitchens : presenting eight food-safe steps : written expressly for the home cook / by Ann Marchiony.
  p. cm.
 ISBN 0-13-112590-7
 1. Food adulteration and inspection—Outlines, syllabi, etc. 2. Food handling—Safety measures—Outlines, syllabi, etc. I. Title.
 TX531 .M33 2003
 641.5'028'9—dc21

                                                  2003005366

"All temperatures given in this book are correct and current with USDA's recommended internal temperatures for consumer use." USDA Meat and Poultry Hotline for consumers— 1-800-535-4555.

This Hotline is staffed by home economists, dietitians, and food technologists on weekdays year 'round from 10 A.M. to 4 P.M. Eastern time. An extensive selection of food safety recordings can be heard 24 hours a day using a touch-tone phone.

**Editor-in-Chief:** Stephen Helba
**Executive Assistant:** Nancy Kesterson
**Executive Acquisitions Editor:**
 Vernon R. Anthony
**Director of Manufacturing**
 **and Production:** Bruce Johnson
**Editorial Assistant:** Ann Brunner
**Managing Editor:** Mary Carnis
**Production Liaison:** Adele M. Kupchik
**Senior Marketing Manager:** Ryan DeGrote
**Production Management:** Pine Tree
 Composition, Inc.
**Production Editor:** John Shannon, Pine Tree
 Composition, Inc.

**Manufacturing Manager:** Ilene Sanford
**Manufacturing Buyer:** Cathleen Petersen
**Creative Director:** Cheryl Asherman
**Senior Design Coordinator:** Miguel Ortiz
**Interior Design:** John Shannon, Pine Tree
 Composition, Inc.
**Printer/Binder:** RR Donnelley & Sons
 Company
**Cover Design:** Marianne Frasco
**Cover Illustration:** Laura Lane, Taxi/Getty
 Images, Inc.; Ryan McVay, PhotoDisc
 Green/Getty Images, Inc.
**Cover Printer:** Phoenix Color

Pearson Education LTD.
Pearson Education Australia PTY, Limited
Pearson Education Singapore, Pte. Ltd
Pearson Education North Asia Ltd

Pearson Education Canada, Ltd.
Pearson Educación de Mexico, S.A. de C.V.
Pearson Education—Japan
Pearson Education Malaysia, Pte. Ltd

10 9 8 7 6 5 4 3 2 1
ISBN 0-13-112590-7

*Food-Safe Kitchens* is lovingly dedicated
to the memory of
Executive Chef Robert J. Chantos
CEC, AAC, CDM, CFPP

# Contents

PREFACE ix

ACKNOWLEDGMENTS xii

INTRODUCTION xvi

DANGER ZONE THERMOMETER xxi


PART ONE    Food-Safe Steps    1

Eight Food-Safe Steps 3
    Food-Safe Step #1    Wash Your Hands; Cleanliness 24/7    3
    Food-Safe Step #2    Before You Shop    7
    Food-Safe Step #3    To Market, To Market    9
    Food-Safe Step #4    Home Again, Home Again    14
    Food-Safe Step #5    Keep a Food Thermometer At-the-Ready    24
    Food-Safe Step #6    Avoid Cross-Contamination    27
    Food-Safe Step #7    Serving Food the Food-Safe Way    28
    Food-Safe Step #8    Leftovers Can Be Dangerous    30


PART TWO    Educational Information    33

The Germs: Their Names, Type and Cause of Illness,
        Common Foods Affected, and the Prevention    35
That '24-Hour Flu'? It Might Be Something You Ate!    39
Everything a Home Cook Should Know About Food Thermometers    41
    Why Use a Food Thermometer?    41
    Color Is Not a Reliable Indiator    42
    Safety versus Doneness    42
    Types of Thermometers    43
    Doneness and Safety    48
    Using the Food Thermometer    48
Label Reading If You Have Food Allergies    53
    Managing a Milk Allergy    54
    Managing an Egg Allergy    55
    Managing a Peanut Allergy    56
    Managing a Tree Nut Allergy    56
    Managing a Fish and/or Shellfish Allergy    57
    Managing a Soy Allergy    58
    Managing a Wheat Allergy    59
    What Is the Difference Between Food Allergy
        and Food Intolerance    59

What Is the Difference Between a Food Allergy
   and a Foodborne Illness?                                    62
      What Is the Difference Between Food Allergy
         and Food Intolerance?                                 63
Drinking Raw Juices Is Dangerous                               65
New Education for Pregnant Women                               67
Teaching Children Food Safety                                  70
Seniors' Food-Safe Alert                                       72
      Good Advice for Both Children and Adults Who Care
         for Their Pets: Use Extra Hygiene                     75
      When You Go Out to Eat                                   75
Do You See What I See?                                         76

## PART THREE      Happy Holidays All Year     **77**

Food-Safe Entertaining                                         79
      Foodborne Infections in the Home Can Be Linked
         to Social Functions                                   80
      Informal Parties/Buffets                                 80
      Consider Leftovers and Storage                           82
Turkey Day Talk                                                83
      Purchasing the Turkey                                    83
      Thawing                                                  83
      Preparing the Bird                                       84
      To Stuff or Not to Stuff                                 84
      Cooking the Turkey from the Frozen State                 85
      Holding the Turkey for Late Arrivals                     86
      Serving the Bird                                         86
      Using the Turkey Meat                                    86
Holiday Foods                                                  87
      Making Holiday Food Gifts                                87
      Christmas/New Year's                                     88
      To Sum Up: Safe Holiday Food                             88
Transporting Food Out of Your Kitchen                          89
      Why Is There a Potential Problem with Potluck Meals?     89
      What Should I Take to a Potluck to Reduce the Risks
         Associated with Foodborne Illness?                    89
Plan a Food-Safe Easter Egg Hunt                               91
Dashboard Dining                                               93
      Traveling with Food                                      94
      Tips for Perishable Foods                                94
      How to Keep Hands and Eating Surfaces Clean Outdoors     95
Great Advice for an Enjoyable and Safe Picnic                  96
Tips on Packing a Safe and Nutritious School Lunch            98

**PART FOUR      Coping with Crises                                    101**

What To Do If You or a Family Member Develops
  a Foodborne Illness                                                  103
What To Do When the Refrigerator Goes Off                             104
Other Kitchen Contaminants                                            107

**PART FIVE      When You Want To Know More                            109**

Contact the Cooperative Extension Office in Your State                111
If You Want To Learn More About Food Safety                           116
  What Causes Foodborne Illness?                                      116
  What Are the Most Common Foodborne Diseases?                        116
  When To Consult Your Doctor About a Diarrheal Illness               118
  How Many Cases of Foodborne Disease Are There
    in the United States?                                             118
  How Do Public Health Departments Track Foodborne
    Diseases?                                                         118
  What Are Foodborne Disease Outbreaks
    and How Do They Occur?                                            119
  How Does Food Become Contaminated?                                  120
  What Foods Are Most Associated with Foodborne Illness?              121
  What Can Home Cooks Do To Protect Their Families
    and Themselves from Foodborne Illness?                            122
  Are Some People More Likely To Contract
    a Foodborne Illness? If So, Are There Special
    Precautions They Should Take?                                     123
  What Can Consumers Do When They Eat in Restaurants?                 123
  How Can Food Be Made Safer in the First Place?                      124
  What Is CDC Doing To Control and Prevent Foodborne
    Disease?                                                          125
  What Are Some Unsolved Problems in Foodborne Disease?               126
  What Is the Microbial Cause of Outbreaks in Which No
    Pathogen Can Be Identified by Current Methods?                    126
Careers Available in Food Safety                                      128

**INDEX                                                                 131**

# *Preface*

Never doubt that a small group of committed people can change the world. Indeed it is the only thing that ever has.

Margaret Mead

It was in 1993, during just another hot summer in Phoenix, when my passion for food safety took root. I was in my third year as Central District President of Arizona Press Women, when a member asked if I would be interested in doing some free-lance writing for *Shamrock Showcase,* a monthly trade magazine of Shamrock Foods Company, a popular local food purveyor. Although busy with my public relations firm, it sounded like fun.

Little did I know that my productive association with Catherine Gervais, the young caring woman publisher, would continue for the next four years. Interviews with some of the top people in Arizona's culinary field gave important contacts that took my career in a whole new direction, changing my life in the process.

One day I was invited to a meeting of a local chefs' group with the long name of Resort & Country Club Chefs Association of the New Southwest, ACF. Here I met their president, Executive Chef Robert J. Chantos, as well as many other professional culinarians.

As my contacts grew, I was encouraged to write for *National Culinary Review,* the official national chef's magazine, as well as a number of other trade publications. No one was ever too busy to give me substantial quotes about the food business that impressed my editors. I became involved in helping promote several food events that Chef Chantos put on for the professionals in his industry.

This is another world, I thought, as I was initiated into the rarified chef community.

I often kidded Chef Chantos, who had worked in the culinary field for more than 33 years as an executive chef, a food service director and a dietary manager, that he had earned as many initials after his name as he had in his name: CEC (Certified Executive Chef), AAC (American Academy of Chefs), CDM (Certified Dietary Manager), and CFPP (Certified Food Protection Professional).

Chef Chantos lived and breathed food safety on a 24/7 basis, shocking some of the most sophisticated serving staffs when he pulled a thermometer from its case in his shirt pocket to check the temperature of the meat he was being served.

As a certified ServSafe trainer and persuasive instructor for the National Restaurant Association's (NRA) food safety program, Chef Chantos raised my consciousness about the seriousness and importance of food safety rules.

In 1996, my husband Bill—the chef in our home—and I enrolled in this two-day course and were certified as Food Protection Managers. Instructor Chantos taught our class about the formidable names of some of the deadly pathogens that cause foodborne illnesses when they enter the food supply, such as *E. coli 0157:H7*.

But, most importantly, Chef Chantos showed us how to prevent these unseen critters from harming us. Well-known for giving unconditionally of his time and expertise, he taught how just a few easy steps could prevent food poisoning—or what is more accurately called foodborne illness. Chef Chantos's passion—that the complete subject of food safety is made available to the home cook—became my passion.

I learned about the four children who died in 1993 after eating contaminated hamburger at one fast-food restaurant in the northwest and the staggering number of 700 children and adults who were infected with *E. coli 0157:H7*. Immediately, I arranged two phone interviews: one with the woman who had documented first hand accounts of the tragedies of the children, who gave me an account too chilling to repeat here.

The other interview was with Dr. David Theno, a highly qualified food-safety expert with 20 years of experience in food safety, quality and technical operations who was brought in by the affected restaurant chain to design a "farm-to-fork" food-safety system that would become the safety standard for the industry and assure that each employee was successfully certified in the National Restaurant Association Educational Foundation's *ServSafe* program.

As all of these experiences unfolded, I was becoming a well-published freelance journalist for a dozen trade publications on the subject of food safety, interviewing talented chefs about the food they prepare and their professional kitchen equipment and how each of them use their expertise to protect their patrons, patients, students, or inmates from harm on a daily basis. Solid information came from dietitians; equipment and food manufacturers and distributors; farmers; food service directors; nutritionists; produce grocery managers; restaurateurs; and owners of retail specialty gourmet stores.

Some special opportunities were offered me: Colleen Phalen, publisher and editor of *Cooking for Profit* magazine, for whom I'd written, assigned me a monthly column about how chefs and foodservice directors use the seven principles of HACCP (Hazards Analysis Critical Control Points) in preparing safe food in their kitchens.

The NRA's Educational Foundation requested a piece for their January 2001 newsletter that was sent to ServSafe instructors. I was also the only journalist invited to write a chapter in a book by M. Royce Lynch, MS, CFE, entitled "*HACCP—A Chef's Perspective.*"

Chef Chantos firmly believed that the general public must become aware of the gravity of the problem of foodborne illnesses and that it was imperative for every home cook to learn the simple, practical food-safety system used by professional food handlers.

Together, the chef and I decided to get out the urgent word to the people who cook everyday in their own kitchens that an illness they may experience may not be caused by a 24-hour flu, but by something they ate.

The writing of *Food-Safe Kitchens* was begun in 1998, in collaboration with Chef Chantos, until he passed on in September, 2000. I dedicate this book to him.

It is interesting to note that in September 2000, the International Food Information Council (IFIC) published the report below that summarized the findings of qualitative research conducted by Axiom Research Company (now Cogent Research) on behalf of IFIC.

"The purpose of the study was to understand physicians' views of food safety issues and education materials concerning this topic.

"The Executive Summary Dominant Findings: This research indicated that, with very few exceptions, physicians who treat patients at high risk for foodborne illness are not talking about food safety or foodborne illness with these patients. While physicians agreed that foodborne illness can pose a serious threat when patients present the symptoms, they feel that in general providing patients with preventive information in this area is relatively unimportant. In fact, one of the most striking findings in this research was that physicians generally believed that the topic of food safety, and foodborne illness as its main component, is less important than other topics, namely heart health, smoking and drug/alcohol use.

"To sum up here, physicians gave these reasons for not giving food safety information to their patients: limited office visit time: feel patients are "inundated" with health information ("there is just so much patients can absorb"); "It's not my job"—this is a topic that should more appropriately come from "public health" people; and after physicians evaluate health behaviors, they advise accordingly. Specifically, in these groups the obstetrician/gynecologists were least aware of the risks to their patients who were pregnant women and women of childbearing age.

"IFIC concluded at that time that less formal medical information sources, such as magazines and supermarkets are needed as well as easy-to-read material for physician waiting rooms.

"Therefore, IFIC and its partners U.S. Department of Agriculture/Food Safety and Inspection Service; Department of Health and Human Services (Centers for Disease Control and Prevention and the Food and Drug Administration); and the Association of Women's Health, Obstetric and Neonatal Nurses, have developed a patient education piece, *Listeriosis and Pregnancy: What Is Your Risk?,* a concise tear pad to communicate food safety for pregnant women. (Tear Pads can be ordered through IFIC's Web site—http://ific.org.) Perhaps this book, along with the tear pads, will help fill the niche in food safety education."

Now, with the past collaboration of this talented man, and good information from a willing baker's dozen of other skilled professionals in the culinary field, I present this work in the sincere faith that the readers of *Food-Safe Kitchens* will take the easy-to-understand information to heart.

As Chef Chantos often said: "It's a matter of life and death."

Ann Marchiony

# *Acknowledgments*

Every effort has been taken to ensure that the information in this book is accurate and up-to-date. To do this, I asked a group of 13 professional food safety specialists to review this manuscript, give their input and make any necessary corrections, and to add some pearls of wisdom of their own.

These special contributors, whom I affectionately refer to as my "Baker's Dozen," are listed below.

- **Tom Dominick, RS,** Vice President, Food Safety and Sanitation, Bashas', Inc., Chandler, AZ. Bashas' is a family-owned chain of 131 grocery stores under various banners in Arizona, California, and New Mexico. Tom is a registered sanitarian and formerly worked as an Environmental Health Lead Specialist for Maricopa County, AZ. His advice about food shopping is invaluable.

- **Todd Frantz, REHS,** Food Safety Manager, Disneyland Resort, is a past president of the California Environmental Health Association.

- **Dion Lerman,** Food Safety Training, Philadelphia, PA, shared the information about hand washing (courtesy of his company HEALTH MINDER™, A Sloan Valve Co.) that everyone should follow.

- **Executive Chef Steven Linzy, CFSP, FMP, CCE,** Gilbert, AZ, in the foodservice industry for over 30 years, now holds the positions of National Accounts Manager and Program Development Manager Food Safety & Personal Hygiene for Katchall/San Jamar.

- **David F. Ludwig, MPH, RS,** manager, Maricopa County Environmental Services Dept, Phoenix, AZ. Maricopa County is the fourth most populous county in the country as well as the fastest-growing county. The growth challenges coupled with the ever-changing environment in the food arena have forced the county to be innovated. The vision of the Department's Environmental Health Division is to be Arizona's food protection leader and to achieve national recognition as one of the best in the country. In striving to meet their vision, the Maricopa County Environmental Services Department was the recipient of the 2001 Samuel J. Crumbine Consumer Protection Award. The Award denotes the best food safety protection program internationally.

- **Dr. David McSwane,** Associate Professor, Indiana University School of Public and Environmental Affairs, Indianapolis, IN, whose chart on germs that appears in *Food-Safe Kitchens* can be found in the book he coauthored, *Essentials of Food Safety & Sanitation,* Prentice Hall. Dr. McSwane is the recipient of the Walter S. Mangold award, the highest honor bestowed by NEHA. His sincere support is much appreciated.

- **The Food Safety Education Staff, USDA and FSIS Food Safety,** Washington, DC, a talented, tireless group that includes their Hotline lady, who provided great information about turkeys.
- **USDA's Holly Mc Peak,** who became my mentor via e-mail. Actually, it was Holly who first suggested that I write a food safety book just for home cooks. Her constant encouragement has kept me at this year-long task.
- **Ralph Meer, PhD, RD,** with **Scottie Misner, PhD, RD.** The University of Arizona, Department of Nutritional Sciences, Tucson, AZ. Both contributed the important information about how to make picnics safe.
- **L. Charnette Norton, MS, RD, LD, FADA, FCSI,** The Norton Group, Missouri City, Texas, is the co-author of HACCP *The Future Challenge.* The Norton Group, Inc., Publishers, Missouri City, Texas. From the time I began writing about food safety, Char has provided me with important and always accurate information. Over the years, she has become a most knowledgeable friend who always has time for a good interview.
- **Robert W. Powitz, PhD, MPH, RS, DLAAS,** Forensic Sanitarian, Old Saybrook, CT. Dr. Powitz's impressive background includes a Diplomate Laureate, American Academy of Sanitarians; Diplomate of the American Academy of Certified Consultants and Experts; and Diplomate of the American Board of Forensic Engineering and Technology. Dr. Powitz has been very supportive as he has provided only absolutely correct information.
- And my last, but not least, baker's dozen, **Fred Reimers, Manager, Food Safety, H-E-B Food and Drug,** San Antonio, TX. My sincerest thanks for the good input from this busy man.

My special thanks goes to Prentice Hall, publisher of *Essentials of Food Safety & Sanitation,* for permission to use the charts of the causes of foodborne illnesses that appeared in the book written by David McSwane, HSD, Nancy Rue, PhD, and Richard Linton, PhD.

And very special thanks to Dr. Robert Tauxe, Chief of the Foodborne and Diarrheal Diseases Branch, and Centers for Disease Control and Prevention, Atlanta, Georgia, for his final and accurate quote about the 24-hour flu; and to Dr. Michael P. Doyle, Regents Professor and Director, Center for Food Safety, University of Georgia, Griffin, Georgia, for his complete information about sanitizing both kitchens and food.

Also special thanks to my dear friend, June Payne, a retired editor of Arizona State University publications, who many hours of her time to assist me in the final copyediting of this work. To Thelma Pressman, the Pioneer of the Microwave, who gave me permission to use the great old sign about using the electric light.

And thanks to my talented brother-in-law, Larry Marchiony, who, when asked at the 11th hour, instantly put into motion his experience of 25 years in a top advertising firm together with a fine arts degree to produce the drawings of the chefs wearing toques for this project.

My sincere gratitude to the following:

Randy Huffman, Vice President, Scientific Affairs, American Meat Institute Foundation, Arlington, VA for providing clear information about what to look for when buying lamb, pork, and veal.

Pat Devlin, Director, Sales/Marketing, Chaney Instruments, Lake Geneva, WI, for offering support and cooperation.

Mary Alice Gettings, MS, RD, CDE, Pennsylvania State University, Nutrition/Health Agent, Beaver, PA., for providing the information on what to do when the refrigerator goes off.

Cynthia A. Roberts, a faculty member at the Department of Nutrition and Food Science, University of Maryland and the Coordinator of the USDA/FDA Foodborne Illness Education Information Center, Beltsville, MD, who gave permission to use her information for my chapter, Careers Available in Food Safety. Her continuing support is appreciated.

The Food Allergy & Anaphylaxis Network, Fairfax, VA, for explaining how to read labels for people on special diets.

Jay Franks, president, SafetyCheck America, for the quote about new information about flies.

Usha Kalro, Extension Specialist, Nutrition and Health, University of the District of Columbia for doing so much research to help me find a good list for readers to contact Cooperative Extension offices in all 50 U.S states.

And to Ray Kerege, Oro Valley, AZ, who has a Web site called *www.culinaryconnect.com* just for professionals in the culinary field. Ray has sent me lots of encouraging and informative e-mails.

To good friend Emily Rue—the first woman chef in Arizona to become a certified executive chef—for her input about storing food in a home refrigerator.

To Elisa Zied, MS, RD, CDN, a registered dietitian and certified nutritionist, for her good advise about food safety.

To Laura Chantos, widow of Executive Chef Robert J. Chantos, for her full and always welcome support.

To Susan Purdy, cookbook author, and my International Association of Culinary Professional (IACP) mentor, whose supportive e-mails and constructive ideas were the first to encourage me in this long writing journey.

Norma Shaw, my good friend and computer whiz in California. *Food-Safe Kitchens* would have been an impossible task to put on the computer without her ability to put everything in some semblance of order.

My dear friend, June Behrens, who took time from her busy retirement life in sunny Florida to read *Food-Safe Kitchens* from the honest vantage point of a good home cook.

My Arizona Press Woman buddy: Barbara Lacy, who did a fine first read, and June Payne, a retired editor of ASU Publications, who devoted hours of her busy time to assist in the final copyediting of this work.

To daughter Nancy Morris, for her extremely helpful ideas from the point of view of a home cook and for her valuable time to verify some of the important information given in this book.

To daughter Linda Francis, the best cook in the whole family, for her extensive knowledge of the natural way of eating that has sustained me over the many long months of writing.

To granddaughter Trish, better known to me as Precious, and to my grandson Jason, the best music man in this century, for always being proud of me and expressing honest interested in this project.

And, last but never least, to my loving and lovable husband Bill, the cook in our household, for a happy lifetime of continuing loving support and cooperation.

# Introduction

Most people want to do the right thing. They just don't know what it is. There-fore, it follows that we are doing things wrong because we think they are right.

Anonymous

---

*Food-Safe Kitchens* is built on the foundation of Eight Food-Safe Steps. When you follow them in your home kitchen, these eight steps can protect you, your family, and your guests from foodborne illnesses.

And what is foodborne illness? You may call it food poisoning, but by any other name, it can be just as deadly. Are you shocked to learn that most of the time what you thought was the 24-hour flu could have been caused by something you ate? And you could have prepared that food!

According to the Centers for Disease Control and Prevention, each day 200,000 Americans are sickened by a foodborne illness, 900 are hospitalized, and 14 die.

These Eight Food-Safe Steps are listed on the Contents page of this book. Note that in the right column are the page numbers where you may locate the full, easy-to-follow directions for each step. Each of the Eight Food-Safe Steps will appear numerically in Part One.

First, here is a short explanation about how I built these eight steps. Rules to protect food began back in the 1950s when the National Aeronautics and Space Administration (NASA) wanted to ensure that "space foods" that were to be used on manned space flights were 100 percent safe food products. In 1959, Dr. Howard Bauman with the Pillsbury Company discovered that the only way to accomplish this was to establish complete control over the entire process—including the raw materials, the processing environment, and the people involved. Finally, in 1971, at the National Conference on Food Protection, Pillsbury presented a scientifically based system, known by the acronym HACCP (pronounced HASS-SIP), Hazard Analysis Critical Control Point. The HACCP system is now used throughout the country from farmers to chefs. This system is designed to prevent food safety problems before they occur, rather than reacting to any hazards in the finished products.

First the severity and risks of potential hazards are determined, and the critical control points in the food-production process identified. Then procedures are set up to control and monitor these processes. Corrective action is then taken and entered into a record-keeping system. While every employee of a professional kitchen must adhere to very firm rules, this complex system is not necessary for the home cook who prepares only a few meals a day.

However, everyone preparing food should follow these basic principles to prevent foodborne illnesses: assure hands are properly washed, foods and cooking utensils are properly washed, hot foods kept hot and cold foods kept cold; and cross-contamination is avoided.

In case you are wondering why these eight steps are necessary for you to follow each time you prepare any food in your kitchen, meet Nancy Donley from Chicago, Illinois.

On a pleasant July day in 1993, Nancy Donley, a caring mother, cooked a hamburger for her only son in their own backyard. Unknown to her, the hamburger meat was contaminated with cattle feces. Within four days, Nancy and Tom Donley's son Alex, after unbelievable agony, was dead at the age of six. The cause was *E. coli 0157: H7,* one of the hundreds of strains of pathogens that enter the food supply and cause foodborne illnesses.

**This tragedy could have been prevented with the simple and proper use of a food thermometer.**

"I had never heard the term *E.coli,* nor did I know that hamburger meat bought in a reputable store could be contaminated," said Nancy Donley. "Too late I realized I had committed the monumental error that many, many consumers commit. I assumed," she stressed. "We always assume that the food we buy in our grocery stores or eat in our restaurants is safe.

"If I had used a food thermometer," admits Donley, "I could have saved our son's life. Now I tell everyone that hamburger must be cooked to 160 degrees F. for 15 seconds to kill the bacteria that cause foodborne illness and death.

"The old rules don't apply," warns Donley. "Do not use your finger to press on the gray-colored meat to determine if the meat is done. Know that the aroma, appearance, heat radiation, or brownness do not ensure that bacteria are killed. The only way to be sure is to check the inside temperature of the food with a thermometer."

As this book was being written, someone told me that most people are more interested in nutrition than in food safety. With that logic, from a nutritional point of view, the protein lunch Nancy Donley cooked for her son should have been good for him. But consider that since the meat purchased at her local supermarket contained fecal material, a fatal pathogen was present. The bacteria's toxins liquefied portions of Alex's brain, and none of his organs could be donated.

But that happened years ago, you say. Isn't our food safer now? While pathogens in meat products have been reduced, and consumers are more knowledgeable, the threat of foodborne illnesses at our own hands or the hands of others still exists. The time has come for every home cook to take some easy-to-understand steps to prevent foodborne illnesses. We can never be too safe. This is why I wrote *Food-Safe Kitchens.*

**Let's look at the facts:**

Food has changed more in the past 30 years than in the last 3,000. However, most of us still just eat any food, or serve it, without thinking about what we are eating or how we prepared the food for our family.

Instead, we expect our lawmakers and food-safety experts to handle any and all problems and "fix" them before the food reaches our local markets. Food of every description is now imported into our country, and the general public is not aware that we have barely enough people to inspect our foods grown in America.

**Consider at this writing:**
- The FDA inspects fresh eggs in shells.
- The USDA inspects liquid, frozen, or dried eggs.
- The FDA inspects and ensures the safety of frozen cheese pizza.
- But if there's pepperoni on that pizza, it falls under the jurisdiction of the USDA, as do meat and poultry.
- Dairy, shellfish, and other foods belong to FDA.
- Marine fish, to add one more agency to the mix, are inspected by the National Marine Fishery Service, part of the U.S. Department of Commerce.
- An important issue is the differences between agencies regarding the proper temperatures for foods.

There are moves afoot to put all of these agencies "on one plate." A number of bills have been written and presented by members of the Congress and the Senate to do this. I believe that only when voters, especially those who cook in their own homes, become aware of the urgency of our food safety issues that changes will be made.

Indeed, for all of us, the time has come to become vigilant Americans, to take control and be aware of the best and only way to handle all food brought into our own kitchens so we can serve safe meals to our family and friends.

People who have read *Food-Safe Kitchens* before you have remarked that even the simple steps laid out in *Food-Safe Kitchens* could mean a "lifestyle" change for them. Consider that your lifestyle—your way of life—reflects your attitudes and values and the way things have always been done. Will you consider a change in your understanding if it is for good?

In order to accept new ideas, we all must have the ability to see "outside the box" and give up our preconceived ideas of the way certain things have always been done. Just remember: *That was then; this is now.*

As a nation, we saved lives by becoming aware of the necessity of driving with seat belts and securing very young children in a child's seat in the back of the car attached to the rear seat. This same raising of consciousness applies to being aware of the Eight Food-Safe Steps. Anything less could produce a foodborne illness.

## Tools for the Food-Safe Kitchen
As you become aware that you, as the home cook, and responsible for food preparation in your own home, are the only person who really can ensure food safety in your family. As you learn about these Eight Food-Safe Steps, you may want to seek out some important pieces of equipment for your kitchen:

- Set of four thermometers: one for the freezer, one for the refrigerator, one for the oven, and a meat/food thermometer for food cooked on the top of the stove or on the grill.

- Nailbrush for every sink in your house.
- Set of tongs for picking up hot food.
- One good wooden cutting board or several color-coded cutting boards to be used for the types of food you prepare most often.
- Box of disposable vinyl gloves when a cut or rash is on the hand.
- One pair of reusable heavier Playtex gloves for use in very hot water.

*Food-Safe Kitchens* is divided into five parts and includes an index. You will find in these pages everything that my baker's dozen of food-safety professionals deem important for a home cook to know. I list these invaluable consultants under Acknowledgments in the beginning of the book.

Look for the *Chef's Toque* (chef's hat) throughout the book for great tips and suggestions from professionals who practice food safety every day.

You will find much valuable information within these pages. Some of it you may already know and use. Some you may know but only use when you think of it. You may find some of this information to be strange or unnecessary, or it may not apply to you.

As you read *Food-Safe Kitchens,* you may also realize that some of the information is repeated more than once. Then read what a famous doctor, the inventor of the stereoscope, wrote:

> Do not fear to repeat what has already been said. Men need the truth dinned into their ears many times and from all sides. The first rumor makes them prick up their ears, the second registers, and the third enters.

> René Théophile Hyacinthe LaËnnec (1781–1826),
> Regius Professor of Medicine, College de France

All every professional food-safe specialist asks is that you read this book through one time with the same care and attention you give your loved ones every day. You'll be glad you did. When you practice these basic Eight Food-Safe Steps, you will ensure greater health for your family and you may come to realize that a past illness was, indeed, something you ate!

**A Closing Thought:** Char Norton, one of my baker's dozen food safety experts, has always maintained that the "owner" of the restaurant or head of the hospital, etc., must "buy in" to the entire process of HACCP. Then the staff takes the lead from that head person. "But if that person doesn't pay attention to the rules, they won't either," she says. Therefore, as the head cook in your kitchen, please "buy into" the importance of these Eight Food-Safe Steps. Be sure that they are followed by everyone who enters your kitchen.

According to the U.S. Centers for Disease Control and Prevention (CDC), many people do not think about food safety until a food-related illness affects them or a family member. While the food supply in the United States is one of the safest in the world, the CDC estimates that every year, 76 million people get sick, more than 325,000 are hospitalized, and 5,200 Americans die from a foodborne illness. While young children, pregnant or nursing women, people with impaired immune systems, and the elderly are most susceptible, preventing widespread foodborne illness and death remains a major public health challenge.

The U.S. Centers for Disease Control and Prevention list these six common mistakes as the ones most likely to lead to a food-related illness: inadequate cooling and holding; advance cooking and holding; poor personal hygiene; inadequate reheating; inadequate holding of hot food; and contaminated raw food and ingredients.

The CDC tells us in 2002, the spectrum of foodborne diseases is constantly changing. A century ago, *typhoid fever, tuberculosis,* and *cholera* were common foodborne diseases. *Improvements in food safety,* such as pasteurization of milk, safe canning, and disinfection of water supplies have conquered those diseases. Today other foodborne infections have taken their place, including some that have only recently been discovered. For example, in 1996, the parasite *Cyclospora* suddenly appeared as a cause of diarrheal illness related to Guatemalan raspberries. These berries had just started to be grown commercially in Guatemala, and somehow became contaminated in the field there with this unusual parasite. In 1998, a new strain of the bacterium *Vibrio parahemolyticus* contaminated oyster beds in Galveston Bay and caused an epidemic of diarrheal illness in persons eating the oysters raw. The affected oyster beds were near the shipping lanes, which suggested that the bacterium arrived in the ballast water of freighters and tankers coming into the harbor from distant ports. Newly recognized microbes emerge as public health problems for several reasons: Microbes can easily spread around the world, new microbes can evolve, the environment and ecology are changing, food production practices and consumption habits change, and because better laboratory tests can now identify microbes that were previously unrecognized.

In the last fifteen years, several important diseases of unknown cause have turned out to be complications of foodborne infections. For example, we now know that the Guillain-Barre syndrome can be caused by *Campylobacter* infection, and that the most common cause of acute kidney failure in children, hemolytic uremic syndrome, is caused by infection with *E. coli O157: H7* and related bacteria. In the future, other diseases whose origins are currently unknown may turn out be related to foodborne infections.

***In January, 2003, Dr. Robert Tauxe,*** Chief of the Foodborne and Diarrheal Diseases Branch, and Centers for Disease Control and Prevention ***explains:*** "There is a brief viral GI infection that is intense: The Norwalk virus, and the Norwalk-like viruses. These can be foodborne, or can spread from one person to another more directly. I think that is what people may often be referring to, when they talk about the "GI flu" or the "24-hour flu." It would be most accurate to say: That '24-hour flu'? It might be something you ate!"

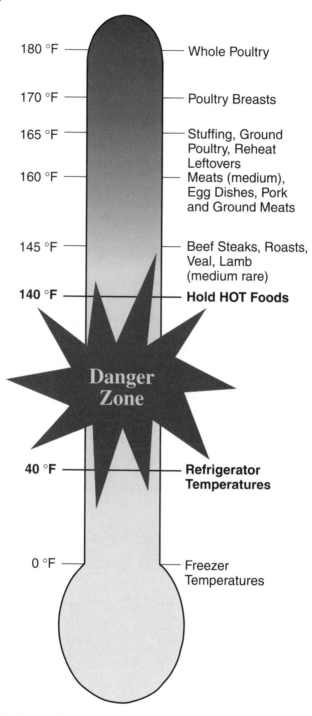

| | |
|---|---|
| 180 °F | Whole Poultry |
| 170 °F | Poultry Breasts |
| 165 °F | Stuffing, Ground Poultry, Reheat Leftovers |
| 160 °F | Meats (medium), Egg Dishes, Pork and Ground Meats |
| 145 °F | Beef Steaks, Roasts, Veal, Lamb (medium rare) |
| **140 °F** | **Hold HOT Foods** |

**Danger Zone**

| | |
|---|---|
| **40 °F** | **Refrigerator Temperatures** |
| 0 °F | Freezer Temperatures |

Used with the permission of the USDA, Food Safety and Inspection Service.

# Food-Safe Kitchens

# PART ONE

# Food-Safe Steps

# Eight Food-Safe Steps

Handwashing is the place to start in order to stop infection. Ask a surgeon!

---

## FOOD-SAFE STEP #1

### Wash Your Hands; Cleanliness 24/7:

Do you wash your hands before you prepare food at home? If not, you are probably among the majority of the U.S. population to violate recommended food safety practices in their own kitchens.

### How to Wash Your Hands

- Use plenty of soap and warm water.
- Clean under your nails with a brush as surgeons do, until they are clean.
- Do a second washing and rinsing without the brush.
- Keep a brush in the kitchen and each bathroom in your house. Give each member of the family his or her own nailbrush. Wash brushes regularly in the dishwasher or clean with soap and water after use. Hang on a convenient hook to air dry.
- Do not try to save time by just wiping your hands on a damp towel.
- Dry hands thoroughly on a disposable paper towel to avoid chapped hands. Washing hands often does not cause your hands to chap. Not wiping your hands until they are completely dry is the cause of chapped hands.

**When to Wash Your Hands**

- Anytime your hands are dirty.
- Before beginning any food preparation.
- Immediately after each food preparation.
- *Before and after* eating.
- *Before and after* touching or handling foods that do not require cooking.
- *Before and after* your hands touch raw animal foods (poultry, meats, seafood, eggs).
- Properly wash your hands:
  - After you go to the bathroom.
  - After you touch your hair or any part of your body.
  - After you change baby's diaper.
  - After you cough, sneeze, or blow your nose.
  - *Before and after* you have cared for a sick person.
  - After you touch any dirty surfaces (dishes, trash, garbage, soiled bed, clothing, clothes).
  - After touching animals of any kind, especially after children visit a petting zoo or play at the theme park or playground at a fast food restaurant before they eat.
  - After you handle money.
  - After using the telephone.
  - After smoking.

With the advent of large wholesale stores that cater both to restaurants as well as the homemaker, alternatives to chlorine sanitizers are more readily available. I recommend quaternary ammonia (a.k.a. QUAT). It's commonly stocked as a sanitizer for bar glasses. It is an excellent anti-microbial, and at my home, we've gotten into the habit of keeping a spray bottle handy for spraying down the counters/sink after preparing raw foods like poultry. Since it isn't chlorine-based, the over-spray doesn't bleach your clothing either.

**Todd Frantz**

### Executive Chef Steven Linzy

There is one place that children go where it should be mandatory for them to wash their hands before eating: When they visit any fast food restaurant that features a theme park or a playground. Kids get on or in these fun pieces of equipment without anyone realizing that many other children have been there before your child. This is called cross-contamination!

### Jon-Paul Hutchins, Executive Chef, Scottsdale Culinary Institute

There are so many new products on the market that promise sanitation, sterility, safety, and peace of mind that it becomes easy to overlook the common sense applications to create a safe environment in your home.

Unfortunately most of our safety techniques were handed down to us from a loving parent or grandparent who understood less about foodborne illness than we did. So we dismissed the day-after-Thanksgiving diarrhea as just eating and drinking too much, when in reality it resulted from a turkey that was left on the buffet for 4 or 5 hours. The queasiness hours after a cocktail party that surely came from "a bug that's going around at the office" instead of the real culprit, which was the sour cream dip that was stored under the dripping roast in the refrigerator.

All of this aside, there are some things that we were taught that do apply like washing our hands. Mom was right: wash your hands, vigorously, with soap and a hand brush, up to the elbows, with the hottest water you can handle then dry with a clean paper towel. That's it, so simple but so often forgotten. And remember to wash your hands often. If you handle meat, wash your hands, if you touch your face, wash your hands, if you pick up something from the floor, wash your hands, if you touch a door knob (believe it or not a hot-bed of cross-contamination), wash your hands!

Joanne Raleigh, vice president of the Tucel Company, Vermont, which makes fine-quality brushes, said her company made a study of how differently people wash their hands with and without a nail brush.

When you wash your hands without a brush, you will find you have a tendency to wash your hands from side to side—like clapping your hands together. Put a brush in your hands, and you no longer do it that way. Instead, you automatically want to scrub your nails. Our study shows that the area where bacteria grows, under the nails and along side of the hands, a brush is needed to clean here.

## Free Offers to *Food-Safe Kitchens* Readers

Here's an opportunity to get a collection of small prize-winning posters with messages that have shown to significantly increase handwashing rates. These posters contain parodies of well-known literary classics and offer an interesting and amusing way for people to remember to wash their hands.

In a continuing campaign to promote handwashing as a way to combat the spread of infectious diseases, the Allegheny County Health Department in Pittsburgh, PA, makes this offer to the readers of *Food-Safe Kitchens*.

To receive all nine of these posters, simply *mail a postcard* with your name and full address requesting Handwashing Posters to:

Allegheny County Health Dept.
Public Information Office
3333 Forbes Avenue, Room 307
Pittsburgh, PA 15213

**It's in Your Hands**

This free booklet, published in both English and Spanish, has been prepared as a national education initiative to empower consumer to take control of home food safety by the American Dietetic Association.

The booklet advises you to take control of home food safety by following four simple tips: 1) wash hands often; 2) keep raw meats and ready-to-eat foods separate; 3) cook to proper temperatures; 4) refrigerate promptly at 40 degrees F.

To receive a free "It's in Your Hands" brochure, call ADA's Consumer Nutrition Information line at 1-800-366-1655 or send a self-addressed, stamped business-size envelope to:

American Dietetic Association, NCND
Home Food Safety Brochure
216 W. Jackson Blvd.
Chicago, IL 60606

The 70,000-member American Dietetic Association is the largest organization of food and nutrition professionals in the nation. With headquarters in Chicago, it serves the public by promoting optimal nutrition, health, and well-being.

---

### Ripped from the News

It began in August, 2002, when Lane County Public Health Services in Oregon began getting many reports of viral gastroenteritis—more commonly called the stomach flu—from people who had eaten away from home in restaurants.

Then, between August 13 and 18, so many people were found to be infected with *E. coli* bacteria that the Lane County Public Health officials declared it was the biggest outbreak of the bacteria in Oregon's history.

"Of the 42 reported cases, 26 involve people under age 18," said Karen Gillette, program manager for Lane County Public Health. "The oldest is 38; the youngest is one year. The source was narrowed to the petting zoo at the ongoing Lane County Fair."

A two-year-old girl wound up in the intensive care unit at Doernbecher Children's Hospital in Portland. The *E. coli* infection caused her kidneys to stop working, so her blood must be tested every six hours; she's fed intravenously and has undergone two rounds of dialysis. Two more children were admitted Tuesday, bringing to five the number of children hospitalized there. All were treated for kidney failure.

According to Dr. Sarah Hendrickson, Lane County Public Health officer, "There have been similar outbreaks here in the Northwest associated with undercooked hamburger, with raw milk consumption, with swimming lakes and day care centers, in addition to petting zoos. We are well-prepared to investigate a communicable disease emergency of this sort."

"If you or your family became ill after visiting the Fair with symptoms including diarrhea and abdominal cramps, consult your family doctor," Dr. Hendrickson advised. "Avoid over-the-counter anti-diarrheal agents, such as Ioperamide (Imodium) and avoid taking antiboiotics because these medicines may increase the risk of complications.

"The key to not getting sick is to keep germs out of your child's mouth. Children should always wash their hands before putting their hands in their mouth. Everyone should wash their hands before eating and after going to the bathroom. Proper hand washing means using plenty of plain soap and water, then rub your sudsy hands all over for at least 15 seconds and rinse well."

The Lane County Fair officials have taken steps to prevent illnesses at the animal barns. Five handwashing stations were in place during this August Fair so fairgoers can wash their hands with soap and water after visiting the animals. However, Dr. Hendricksen and the Fair officials agree that the most effective measure may simply be to increase the public awareness about the importance of handwashing after coming in contact with the animals.

The update of this story is that the Fair faces a possible lawsuit. At least 73 people have become sick from *E. coli O157: H7* linked to an animal barn, including 12 children hospitalized for treatment of a serious complication of *E. coli* infection. A handful of their families have contacted a Seattle law firm that has won numerous multimillion-dollar awards and settlements in *E. coli* cases across the nation. However, under Oregon law, the most any single family could recover from the fair, a public agency, is $200,000, and it's possible that the fair's total liability from the outbreak would be capped at $500,000.

Dale Hancock, a veterinary epidemiologist at Washington State University and a national expert on *E. coli,* said that if children at the Lane County Fair were allowed to pet or have their fingers suckled by small animals without aggressive efforts to encourage hand washing, "that would be a major problem" adding, "There could even be an issue of negligence unless there was supervised handwashing afterward."

Fair officials installed five portable handwashing stations outside animal barns for this year's fair. But they posted no signs warning fairgoers to wash their hands after visiting animals.

## FOOD-SAFE STEP #2

### Before You Shop:

Clean and Sanitize Your Kitchen

A clean kitchen is a safe and healthy kitchen. It is important to take time to prepare your kitchen to accept the wonderful products you will bring home from your food-shopping trip.

### Executive Chef Steven Linzy

It is important to understand the difference between cleaning and sanitizing. These are two different jobs and are a two-step process. *Cleaning* is done first and is a process of removing food and other types of soil from all surfaces from a plate to a countertop by cleaning with hot soapy water and rinsing all surfaces thoroughly. *Sanitizing,* done after the surfaces are clean to the eye, is the process of reducing the number of microorganisms on any surface to a safe level. To sanitize, use a solution of one teaspoon of unscented household bleach in one quart of tap water.

Keep all of the kitchen surfaces, the equipment and utensils that touch any food during preparation, cooking and serving clean and sanitized. Without a dish washer, use heavier nondisposable gloves to do these tasks so you can use very hot water.

Use your dishwasher to sanitize pots, utensils, and other items that have come into contact with food. To handwash: If you don't have a dishwasher, or if you have oversized pots that don't fit in the dishwasher, handwash these items in hot soapy water and allow them to air-dry.

Monitor the temperature of the refrigerator and the freezer regularly.

- Be sure the thermometer in your refrigerator remains no higher than 40 degrees F and frequently check the freezer to see that the temperature stays at 0 degrees F or below.
- Clean and organize the refrigerator. Clean the salad drawers before putting in new produce so that you'll never find moldy, rotting, unrecognizable things at the bottom. Empty the drawers completely and wipe with a clean disposable paper towel. When necessary, wash with hot soapy water and dry well with a disposable paper towel.

### Executive Chef Emily Rue

This is how I organize my home refrigerator. Top shelf: half is for dairy (such as sour cream, yogurts, cottage cheese, butter, etc.), the other half is for cooked foods, leftovers, etc. Second shelf: eggs on one side; juice, milk, etc. on the other side. Always on the bottom—raw meat, that I put into a large plastic container.

- This is a good time to check the dates on the cans and bottles already on your pantry shelf. Be sure no can is swollen, or has flawed seals, seams, rust, or leaks.
- Do *not* use these foods if the listed date is past the current date when you are checking them. Throw them out, or take them back to the store if just purchased.

### It's Up to You!

While the United States has the world's safest food supply, food still needs to be handled properly. From the farm and sea to your grocery store, all those who handle perishable food—growers, food processors, delivery people, and grocery store personnel—must make every effort to keep all of the cold food at their proper temperature of 40 degrees F and below until you buy them.

### Be Prepared

- Once your food is purchased, it is up to you to make a best effort not to ever break this cold chain, so immediately store the cold foods safely in your refrigerator as soon as you return home.
- Before you leave for food shopping, prepare your vehicle to transport your food safely. Keep a Styrofoam® picnic chest or some type of large insulated container in the trunk of your vehicle. If you have to travel a long way to the store, live in a warm climate, or know you won't be returning home immediately, drop in a refreezable ice packet.
- First take care of all other errands, before going food shopping. Each stop takes precious time and a number of "quick" errands always takes far more minutes than you plan. Always go to the grocery store last.

### A Study Has Found New Fly Pathogens

There is nothing new about the knowledge that flies are capable of transmitting disease; that knowledge is centuries old. What we must focus on, however, is dealing with significant hazards based on the likelihood of occurrence and the severity of the risk. Badly handled garbage is one of the problems.

If we could just get the basics accomplished: hot food hot, cold food cold, verified cooking temps, good sanitation, handling and hygiene, a significant percentage of foodborne illnesses goes away. Poof! To handle the flies, keep close-fitting doors shut and regularly hose down the garbage cans, if possible.

**Jay Franks, Safety Check America**

## FOOD-SAFE STEP #3

### To Market, To Market:

Shop With Your Nose and Eyes. Always Read the Labels!

Be alert! Shop efficiently, using all of your senses. As you enter your grocery store or supermarket, be constantly aware of the following:

### Smells

- A store that smells like a hamster cage may have a rodent problem.
- Avoid stores with any strong odors, as they may have sanitation issues that suggest underlying health challenges.
- Strong fish smells may indicate low-quality products or poor sanitation practices.

- The fish department should remind you of fresh sea breezes.
- Don't buy anything that smells bad—with the exception of limburger cheese!
- Be aware of spoiled milk in the dairy case.

### Sights

- Notice the overall cleanliness of the store, especially at the meat, poultry, dairy, and fish counters and the salad bar.
- If the meat department has added spice coatings to any meats, you should question the freshness of the product.
- Water stains on the boxes of frozen fish, chicken nuggets, etc. indicate the food inside has been partially defrosted.
- Check the "sell by" or "use by" date on all packages. If it has today's date on it, and you don't plan to use it for several days, pass it by or freeze immediately. However, just because today's date is the "sell by" date doesn't mean it is an old product. Some stores grind beef fresh many times a day and only allow a "sell by" date of 24 hours or less.

### Food Product Dating

Dates are printed on many food products. After the date expires, is it necessary to discard the food? In most cases, no, as a calendar date may be stamped on a product's package to help the store determine how long to display the product for sale. It is *not* a safety date!

To clearly understand the product dating system, here is a list to watch for:

- **Product dating** is not required by federal regulations although dating of some foods is required by more than 20 states.
- **Calendar dates** are found primarily on perishable foods such as dairy products, eggs, meat, and poultry.
- **Coded dates** might appear on shelf-stable products such as cans and boxes of food.
- **Sell-by date** is the last recommended day of sale, but allows for use in home storage. The date is given after the words "Sell-by." Baked goods and breads may have sell-by dates, also. This tells the store how long to display the product for sale. You should buy the product before the date expires.
- **Use-by date** tells how long the product and some packaged goods will retain top quality after purchase. This is the last date recommended for the use of product while at peak quality. The date has been determined by the manufacturer of the product and is recommended for best flavor or quality. It is not a purchase or safety date.
- **Expiration date:** This is the last day the product should be eaten or used. Also may state "do not use by" (after the date marked). Watch for the expiration date for eggs.

- **Pack date:** Canned or packaged foods could have dates to tell you when the product was processed, but they do *not* tell how long the food will be good.
- **Closed or Coded dates** are packing numbers for use by the manufacturer in tracking their products. This enables manufacturers to rotate their stock as well as locate their products in the event of a recall.

Randy Huffman, Vice President, Scientific Affairs, American Meat Institute Foundation, says that as a consumer buying meat products, you only have a few tools to work with beside checking the dates: color, odor, and feel of the products. Here are his suggestions about:

- **Beef:** Select beef with a bright cherry-red color and no grayish or brown blotches.
- **Lamb:** Look for a brighter cherry-red color.
- **Pork:** Look for pinkish color—typical of fresh pork.
- **Veal:** A bit lighter in color, not quite as pink as pork.

"These types of meat are primarily red meat and meat products that come from cattle (beef), calves (veal), hogs (ham, pork, and bacon), sheep (mutton) and young sheep (lamb). Look for meat that is firm to the touch, not soft. Make sure the package is cold and has no holes or tears. Choose packages without excessive liquid. Purchase all meats before the 'sell-by' date.

"In the case of odor or feeling the meat, you probably would have to wait until you get home to check this as you are rewrapping the meat. If the meat is not good, it may develop a slimy texture on the surface that is characteristic of spoilage. My mom always said 'never eat slippery meat.'"

### Chicken:

Look for "sell-by" or "use-by" date. Pass up any packages with unusual aroma or if you see liquid in package.

- **Look for the grade**
  - Buy U.S. Grade-A poultry.
  - Bone-in products are fully fleshed and meaty, have a normal shape, are free of disjointed or broken bones.
  - Products with the skin on are free of pinfeathers, exposed flesh, and discolorations.
  - Boneless products are free of bone, cartilage, tendons, bruises.
- **Look for the class**
  - The name suggests the cooking method.
  - Young poultry for all cooking methods: broiler, fryer, roaster, capon, Cornish game hen, or the word "young."

- Mature poultry for moist-heat cooking: hen, fowl, stewing or baking chicken, or the words "mature" or "old." The name suggests the cooking method.

### Fresh Fish

- Fresh fish is always glistening.
- Look for fish displayed in a case on a thick bed of fresh ice.
- If you are buying a whole fish, make sure it has red gills, shiny skin, and clear, bulging eyes.
- Be sure that the flesh springs back when pressed.
- Never buy cooked shrimp if it is laying on the same bed of ice as raw fish. *This is called cross-contamination.*
- Cooked and raw seafood, meat, and poultry should never be placed together but should be placed on separate display plates.
- Frozen seafood should be rock-solid and free of ice crystals that indicate the seafood was thawed and refrozen.
- Look to see there are no white spots that indicate freezer burn.
- Look for signs that the fish juices have been thawed. Do not buy previously thawed and refrozen fish. An indication is ice crystals in the package.
- Buy seafood last. If you're going to be delayed, pack fresh fish in a cooler on ice for the ride home in the car.

### Other Foods

- **Glass jars:** Check safety seal button (pop-up tops) on glass jars with metal lids (jelly, spaghetti sauce, etc.) to make sure none have popped.
- **Dry foods:** Check that rice packages do not have small holes that indicate insect infestation. Little moths in the flour, cake mix, or dog food aisles are an indication of Indian meal moth activity—but they don't cause illness.
- **Salad bars:** Avoid fruits and vegetables sold at the store's salad bar if they look brownish, moldy, slimy, or dried-out. These are signs that the product has been held at an improper temperature for too long.
- **Fresh fruits and vegetables:** Every reputable grocery store strives to display only the freshest produce, so change stores if you find fruits and vegetables that are bruised, shriveled, moldy, or slimy.
- **Packaged vegetables:** Don't buy packaged vegetables that have a lot of liquid in the bag or appear slimy. Some bags of fruits, such as precut pineapple, will have liquid in the bag, which is OK.
- **Frozen foods:** Notice the temperature of frozen food cases. Pay attention to temperature of cold/frozen foods before purchasing. If package is very frosty, the case was probably on defrost for too long. Beware of over-

stocked cases as the top food items may have begun to defrost. Frozen vegetable or fries packages with sunk-in tops indicate partial defrosting of these foods. Check that contents are individually frozen or can easily be broken apart. Solid frozen packages indicate defrosting. Peas, for example, should move freely in the bag.

- **Ice cream:** Containers are typically slightly overfilled. If there are spaces at the top of the package, the ice cream has partially melted.
- **Canned goods:** Look out for swollen cans, dented seams or ends, dents (not on seams) resulting in sharp points and rust.
- **Baby food:** Infant formula is regulated and must meet the nutritional value on its label. After the "sell-by" date, there is a "mandatory" removal of product from the shelves. *Check the date anyway!*
- **Produce that requires refrigeration:** Some produce cases contain foods that require refrigeration, such as tofu, bean sprouts, alfalfa sprouts, cut melon, etc. Often, produce cases aren't designed to handle these foods, so be careful to check that these foods are cold before you purchase them.
- **Pasteurization:** Buy only pasteurized milk, cheese, juices, and cider. Some people prefer these products unpasteurized, but be sure to locate a Certified Raw Dairy in your area and buy it direct from the company; keep under refrigeration.
- **Eggs:** Choose grade-A or -AA eggs from the refrigerated section and be sure shells are clean and uncracked.
- **Delicatessen department:** Hot perishable foods picked up from the deli department need to be kept warm and consumed within two hours. If you purchase hot deli foods to eat at a later time, place the food in small portions in shallow containers in small portions and refrigerate or freeze as soon as possible.
- **Be sure to mark the date purchased on a removable label:** Perishable foods should be kept at room temperature no longer than two hours.

### Add to Your Grocery Basket or Cart in This Manner

- First, off-the-shelf dry and canned items.
- Next, fruits and vegetables—these are not "stock-up" items. Nutrient content of produce diminishes over time after it has been separated from the plant or the ground. It is better to purchase smaller qualities on a more frequent basis.
- Most items should be used within a few days. Ask the produce manager to help you choose an item with which you're unfamiliar. Request a taste of that vegetable or fruit and ask for care/handling information and a recipe.

### Buy Last

- Perishable items from the refrigerated section, such as deli items, meat, poultry, fish, cheese and dairy.

• Frozen foods. Always put these products in separate plastic bags so that drippings don't contaminate other foods in your shopping cart.

At this point, go immediately to the checker. Don't put uncovered raw items directly on the check-out conveyor belt. Be sure that the checker puts the refrigerated and frozen items in a separate bag or bags. When you go to your car, these items are already separated and immediately can go easily into the ice chest you have there. Better still, why not take your ice chest into the store with you? *Now, please go straight home.*

## FOOD-SAFE STEP #4

### Home Again, Home Again:

Don't Wait—Refrigerate!

#### Beware Not to Break the Cold Chain

Don't get into a conversation with your neighbor or stop to check your answering machine while the cold foods are heating up in the grocery bags. Remember not to put these bags or any other items on your clean counters!

---

**An Experiment with Two Shopping Carts**

Bashas' Markets in Maricopa County, Arizona, put together a revealing study in cooperation with the Maricopa County Health Department, to prove the importance of keeping foods in the *safe* temperature zones: Two shopping carts were placed side by side in the store, each containing an order of one raw, whole chicken and a gallon of milk. However, they were handled two different ways.

The first cart: A chicken (30 degrees F.) and a carton of milk (39 degrees F.) were placed in this shopping cart. The items were left in the cart for one hour to simulate the items being purchased at the start of a shopping trip. After one hour, the chicken was 37 degrees F. and the milk 44 degrees F. Then the items were placed in the trunk of a car (outside temp 98 degrees F. cool for Phoenix in June) for one hour. Now the temperature of the chicken was 61 degrees F. and the milk was 66 degrees F. These items were then placed in a home-style refrigerator to cool them back down. The temperature of the chicken was in the temperature danger zone (TDZ) for 4.5 hours and the milk for 5.5 hours. In a restaurant or a supermarket, the requirement by law is to discard any food that has been in the TDZ for more than 4 hours.

The second cart: Another chicken (33 degrees F.) and two gallons of milk (39 degrees F.) were placed in a shopping cart for about 10 minutes to simulate these items being purchased right before check-out. The items were placed in a cooler with ice packs in the car trunk. After one hour, the chicken was actually colder at 32 degrees F. and the milk was 41 degrees F. Neither product spent any time in the temperature danger zone.

---

# Chicken from Cart to Kitchen

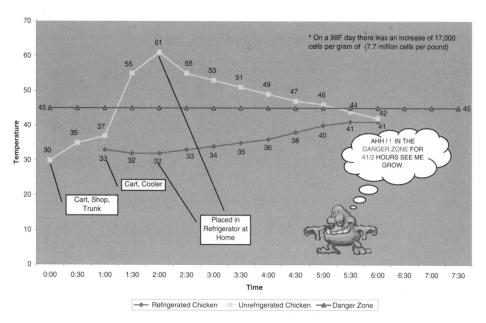

# Milk from Cart to Kitchen

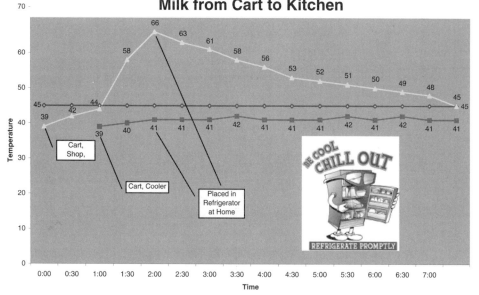

### First, Wash Your Hands!

Then set about unpacking and properly storing all foods in your freshly cleaned kitchen. See page 17 for information about proper refrigerator storage that is the key to longer-lasting fruits, meats, and vegetables.

### Steps to Unpack

- First put away the cold and frozen items; next store meat, fish, poultry, eggs; then fresh fruits and vegetables in the refrigerator.
- Freeze meat and poultry if not planning to use within 2 to 3 days. Freeze seafood if it's not to be used by the next day.
- Store all cut fruits and vegetables in the refrigerator.
- Keep most of your produce in the crisper where there is a slightly higher humidity level than the rest of the refrigerator, which is better for fruits and vegetables.

### Extra Tip from Our Forensic Sanitarian Dr. Powitz

"Washing produce before storing is a no-no. Water on the produce encourages spoilage bacteria (an example of this is storing strawberries after washing) . . . as well as the growth of a pathogen or two. Remember, all pathogenic and most spoilage organisms grow best when wet. I have never been an advocate for extended home storage of any fresh foods (excluding root crops). Treat raw leafy vegetables as you would fresh fish and you can't go wrong. My advice has always been: buy fresh and prepare fresh."

---

#### For Your Special Attention

While you were grocery shopping, you carefully checked each product for the DATES. Now it is your turn to DATE, as the chefs do, most of your refrigerated and frozen items. None of the storage containers that we have found on the market, offer you, the home consumer, a way to DATE your foods. Therefore, we suggest, until one of these companies gets smart and sells labels with their containers, that you pick up a package of peel-and-stick labels at your local stationery store. Considering that foods *should not be kept more than three days after removed from original containers or after original preparation,* write your use-by date on the label—do the math and add 2 to 3 days to the date. Keep these labels at-the-ready to place on each container after the food is stored inside. Be sure to take the label off before the container is put in the dishwasher.

---

There are three categories of fruits and vegetables:

| Don't refrigerate | Store: warmest area | Store: coldest area |
|---|---|---|
| avocados | berries | apples |
| bananas | citrus fruits | asparagus |
| pickling cucumbers | fresh corn on cob | broccoli |
| tomatoes | snap beans | leafy greens |
| tropical fruit | | lettuces |

*Reevaluate your refrigerator.*   The position of foods on the refrigerator shelves should be carefully planned when storing food to prevent cross-contamination (the term used when harmful bacteria cross from one surface to another or from one food to another (see Food-Safe Step #6, page 27).

A crisper(s) offers moderate to cool temperature and is the obvious place for things you want to stay crisp: vegetables such as asparagus, broccoli, celery, all leafy greens—use paper towels to make sure all are completely dry—and cheeses wrapped in plastic wrap.

### Store in coolest part—*the back*—of refrigerator

Top shelf: front—eggs in the carton; butter stored in butter dish.

Middle shelves: prepared foods and leftovers (*date* tightly wrapped packages or tight-lid containers).

Bottom shelf: in leak-proof *dated* plastic bag to control juices. *Always* keep all meats and chicken protected to prevent any dripping—and contaminating other foods. Prepare a deep container with a zipper-lock bag full of ice and store fish and shellfish on top.

Cover all foods to prevent cross-contamination, drying out, and the absorption of smells. *Plastic film is useful for this purpose, but should not be put over the food until it is cool.*

- Next put away canned goods.
- Then store cleaning supplies in separate storage area away from all foods you will eat.

### Remember: Wash Produce *Just Before* You Use It, *Not* When You Put It Away

When you are ready to use your produce, handle it properly. The most important thing you can do is wash all fruits and vegetables under clean running tap water just before eating, *not* when the produce is refrigerated.

This applies to all fruits and vegetables, even if you don't eat the rind or skin (such as melons, lemons, oranges and limes). Never cut into a melon until the rind is sanitized. Before cutting the citrus fruit to squeeze into a beverage, wash in the same manner.

Fresh produce can be expected to carry a wide variety of microorganisms, some which may be harmful. Dirt, containing microorganisms, readily attaches to unsmooth surfaces and in the grooves and crevices of vegetables and fruit. Placing vegetables and fruit in a bowl of cold water will not effectively remove the dirt.

An effective method is to wash fruit separately under cold running water and, when appropriate, scrubbing with a brush. Illness caused by these types of microorganisms can be quite serious, especially in young children, the elderly and anyone with a weakened immune system.

Raw fruits and vegetables can become contaminated in their natural environment, and also by people whose hands are not clean when they handle the produce. On average, four other people have handled an apple before you chose it; up to 20 people may have handled your tomato. Raw fruit and vegetables can also be contaminated by a person coughing or sneezing, or if it falls to the floor and is put back on display. The only way to ensure your vegetables are clean is to wash them with cold running water.

---

**Ripped from the News:**

Several years ago, an outbreak in central Indiana of *E.coli O157:H7* affected 27 people and was associated with cabbage coleslaw. Health officials found a food handler missed a critical step by not washing the cabbage prior to processing.

---

***Washing fruits and vegetables:***   Here are steps to follow when preparing raw vegetables and fruit: Don't use detergent or bleach when washing produce as these items are porous and can absorb the chemicals.

- Discard outer leaves of leafy vegetables such as lettuce and cabbage. Break apart leafy produce and wash each piece individually.
- Scrub the outside of melons with water before cutting through the rind. Rinse thoroughly.
- Rub whole items such as apples or tomatoes by hand with a paper towel after washing them.
- Carrots, potatoes, and other root crops should be scrubbed with a vegetable brush or peeled.
- Break apart vegetables that have tight heads, such as broccoli or cauliflower, before washing.
- Cut vegetables and fruit on a clean board or surface—not one that was just used for raw meat. Be sure to use a clean knife.

Most vegetables do well in a plastic bag. Store mushrooms in a paper bag. Don't leave vegetables uncovered in your refrigerator as the cool air tends to have a drying effect on them.

- FIFO stands for First In First Out: Put last week's produce on the top. Use it up before you start using this week's purchases. Example: if you have a new bag of carrots and three carrots left over from last week's shopping, to avoid waste, use those three before you open the new bag.
- Wash tops and bottoms of all food cans before storing, using the FIFO method. Dry thoroughly if you live in a humid area where they could rust.

In addition to washing, before serving, peel and discard outer leaves or rinds. Use a soft brush to scrub hearty vegetables, such as potatoes and carrots, if you plan to eat the fiber and nutrient-rich skin.

NEW Product: Grapefruit Seed Extract is being used to wash all types of produce as well as sinks, counters, and cutting boards, requiring only up to 30 drops in a sink full of water. There are several products on the market containing this extract that can be found in upscale grocery stores and health food stores around the country.

However, here is a strong caution regarding disinfectants and sanitizers from one of our Baker's Dozen, Dr. Robert Powitz, a forensic sanitarian:

"Watch that products that are considered disinfectants and sanitizers, carry an EPA label. Such products fall under the Federal Insecticide, Fungicide and Rodenticide Act that includes all biocidal agents including disinfectants and sanitizers. The act mandates that every biocide should carry an EPA number, verifiable biocidal claims, use and health effects on the label."

### *When to Refrigerate:*

- A few produce items do ***not*** require refrigeration. In fact, refrigeration, in some cases, speeds up the deterioration process or has a negative impact on the taste or color of the produce.
- Garlic, potatoes, and uncut onions (exception: scallions or green onions) are happier tucked away in a cool, dark corner.
- Be sure to clean surfaces, utensils, and your hands *after* touching raw meat and poultry and *before* you touch fresh produce.
- **Beware:** Don't risk getting germs on your produce by letting it come in contact with raw meat/poultry/fish juices or raw eggs. Cover/refrigerate produce you have cut. Don't store raw meats above uncovered fresh produce (this will prevent raw meat juices from dripping on fresh produce). Always wash your hands under running using soap and rinse thoroughly after each task.
- Read and follow label instructions, such as "keep refrigerated" or "use by (a certain date)." Keep prepared fruit salads and other cut produce items in the refrigerator until just before serving. Discard cut produce items if they have been out of the refrigerator for two hours or more.
- **Storing canned hams:** Some canned hams are shelf-stable. However, if hams or any foods are labeled "keep refrigerated," don't put in the pantry. Do as the instructions tell you: refrigerate.

**Recommended Times for Refrigerator and Freezer Food Storage**
Courtesy: Clemson University, Clemson, SC

| Food | Refrigerator | Freezer |
|---|---|---|
| DAIRY | | |
| Fresh milk | 5–7 days | * |
| Buttermilk | 1–2 weeks | * |
| Canned milk (opened) | 3–5 days | * |
| Cream (unwhipped) | 10 days | * |
| Cream (whipped) | 1 day | 2 months |
| Sour cream | 4 weeks | * |
| Yogurt, cottage cheese | 7 days (after "sell-by date") | * |
| Hard cheese, grated cheese | 6–12 weeks | 6–12 months |
| Cheese spreads | 3–4 weeks | * |
| Butter/margarine | 2 weeks | 9 months |
| Ice cream | * | 2 months |
| EGGS | | |
| Fresh in shell | 3 weeks | * |
| Hard cooked | 1 week | * |
| MEATS, FRESH | | |
| Beef roasts, steaks | 3–5 days | 6–12 months |
| Chicken or turkey, pieces | 1–2 days | 9–12 months |
| Chicken or turkey, whole | 1–2 days | 1 year |
| Duck or goose | 1–2 days | 6 months |
| Game birds | 1–2 days | 6 months |
| Giblets | 1–2 days | 3–4 months |
| Ground meat or stew | 1–2 days | 3–4 months |
| Lamb, roasts or chops | 3–5 days | 6–9 months |
| Pork, roasts or chops | 3–5 days | 4–6 months |
| Pre-stuffed pork and lamb chops or chicken breasts | 1 day | * |
| Sausage | 1–2 days | 1–2 months |
| Variety meats: heart, liver, tongue, etc. | 1–2 days | 3–4 months |
| Venison, roasts, steaks, chops | 3–5 days | 6–12 months |
| MEATS, COOKED | | |
| Smoked breakfast sausage | 7 days | 1–2 months |
| Whole ham (fully cooked) | 7 days | 1–2 months |
| Half ham (fully cooked) | 3–5 days | 1–2 months |
| Ham slices (fully cooked) | 3–4 days | 1–2 months |
| Canned ham ("keep refrigerated" label) | 6–9 months | * |
| Hotdogs, luncheon meats (unopened) | 2 weeks | 1–2 months |
| Hotdogs, luncheon meats (opened) | 3–7 days | 1–2 months |
| Cooked, leftover meat | 3–4 days | 2–3 months |
| Leftover gravy and meat broth | 1–2 days | 2–3 months |
| Cooked, leftover poultry | 3–4 days | 4–6 months |

**Recommended Times for Refrigerator and Freezer Food Storage**
Courtesy: Clemson University, Clemson, SC

| Food | Refrigerator | Freezer |
|---|---|---|
| Cooked, leftover chicken nuggets or patties | 1–2 days | 1–3 months |
| SEAFOOD, FRESH | | |
| Fresh lean fish: cod, flounder, trout, haddock, halibut, pollack, perch | 1–2 days | 4–6 months |
| Fresh fatty fish: mullet, smelt, salmon, mackerel, bluefish, tuna and swordfish | 1–2 days | 2–3 months |
| Live crabs and lobster | same day purchased | * |
| Live mussels and clams | 2–3 days | * |
| Live oysters | 7–10 days | * |
| Shucked mussels and clams | 1–2 days | 3–4 months |
| Shucked oysters | 5–7 days | 3–4 months |
| Shrimp, crabmeat | 2–3 days | 4 months |
| Scallops | 2–3 days | 3 months |
| COOKED FISH | | |
| Fish sticks | * | 18 months |
| Bread shrimp, commercial | * | 1 year |
| Cooked pieces | 3–4 days | 3 months |
| FRUITS, FRESH | | |
| Apples | 1 month | 8–12 months |
| Apricots, grapes, nectarines, peaches, pears, plums | 3–5 days | 8–12 months |
| Avocados | 3–5 days | 8–12 months |
| Bananas, plantains | * | 8–12 months |
| Berries, cherries | 2–3 days | 8–12 months |
| Grapefruit, lemons, limes, oranges | 2 weeks | 4–6 months |
| Guavas, papayas | 1–2 days | 8–12 months |
| Kiwis | 3–5 days | 4–6 months |
| Mangoes | * | 8–12 months |
| Melons | 1 week | 8–12 months |
| Pineapple | 2–3 days | 4–6 months |
| VEGETABLES, FRESH | | |
| Artichokes | 1 week | * |
| Asparagus | 2–3 days | 8–12 months |
| Beets, carrots | 2 weeks | 8–12 months |
| Beans, broccoli, lima beans, peas, summer squash | 3–5 days | 8–12 months |
| Cauliflower | 1 week | 8–12 months |
| Cilantro, parsley | 2–3 days | * |
| Corn | use immediately for best flavor | 8–12 months |
| Green onions | 3–5 days | * |
| Celery, cabbage, chilies, green beans, peppers, tomatoes | 1 week | 8–12 months |
| Greens: collards, kale, mustard, spinach, Swiss chard | 3–5 days | 8–12 months |
| Lettuce and salad greens | 1 week | * |

**Recommended Times for Refrigerator and Freezer Food Storage**
Courtesy: Clemson University, Clemson, SC

| Food | Refrigerator | Freezer |
|------|--------------|---------|
| Mushrooms | 1–2 days | 8–12 months |
| Radishes | 2 weeks | * |
| Squash, hard | * | 8–12 months |
| BAKED PRODUCTS | | |
| BREADS: Store at room temperature. Storing in the refrigerator promotes staling. Use the date as a guide or use within 3 to 7 days. | | |
| Bread, yeast | * | 6–12 months |
| Muffins, rolls, quick breads | * | 2–4 months |
| Pancakes and waffles | * | 1–2 months |
| COOKIES | | |
| Baked | * | 4–6 months |
| Unbaked dough | 2–3 days | 6 months |
| CAKES: Store at room temperature, except for cheesecake. Best used within 3 to 7 days. | | |
| Angel and sponge | * | 4–6 months |
| Cheese | 3–7 days | 4–6 months |
| Fruit | * | 1 year |
| Layer cake (butter cream icing or plain) | * | 6 months |
| PASTRIES: Store at room temperature. Best used within 1 to 3 days. | | |
| Danish | * | 3 months |
| Doughnuts | * | 3 months |
| PIES | | |
| Chiffon pie, pumpkin pie | 1–2 days | 1 month |
| Fruit pie | 1–2 days | 1 year |
| Unbaked fruit pies | * | 8 months |

*Storage here not recommended due to safety or quality issues.

*While this next subject is not a food-safety issue, it is helpful to know.* To ripen fruits (peaches, plums, avocados, etc.) put them in a loosely closed brown paper bag (not a plastic bag). The natural ripening gas they give off will be held around them to help them continue to ripen. You can put a ripe banana or apple in with these fruits to speed the process. Some fruits, such as pineapple, will not ripen after they are picked.

| **Odor Produced by** | **Will Be Absorbed by** |
|----------------------|--------------------------|
| Apples | Cabbage, carrots, celery, figs, onions, meat, eggs, dairy products |
| Avocados | Pineapples |
| Carrots | Celery |
| Citrus | Meat, eggs, dairy products |
| Ginger root | Eggplant |

| Odor Produced by | Will Be Absorbed by |
|---|---|
| Leeks | Figs, grapes |
| Onions | Apples, celery, pears |
| Green onions | Corn, figs, grapes, celery, onions, potatoes |
| Pears | Cabbage, carrots, celery, onions, potatoes |
| Potatoes | Apples, pears |
| Green peppers | Pineapple |
| Strongly scented vegetables | Citrus fruit |

When produce is picked, it continues to live and ripen. During this process—called respiration—the product is generating heat and giving off moisture and gases. This action increases the temperature of the item and causes ripening. Therefore, it is critical to get each item into the best storage environment as soon as possible after you bring it home from the store.

***Ethylene gas is one of the most active plant hormones.*** Most fruit and vegetables generate ethylene. *It is required for the ripening process.* However, it can cause damage to leafy vegetables in even very low quantities. For example, when lettuce is exposed to small amounts of ethylene gas at low temperatures—such as in the refrigerator—the product will decay.

Below is a list that shows the items that create ethylene gas and those that are damaged by it.

| Create Ethylene Gas | Damaged by Ethylene Gas |
|---|---|
| Apples | Asparagus |
| Apricots | Belgian endive |
| Avocados | Broccoli |
| Bananas, ripening | Brussels sprouts |
| Blueberries | Cabbage |
| Cantaloupe | Carrots |
| Cherimoya | Cauliflower |
| Citrus fruits (except grapefruit) | Chard |
| Cranberries | Cucumbers |
| Figs | Cut flowers |
| Guavas | Eggplant |
| Grapes | Endive |
| Green Onions | Escarole |
| Honeydew | Florist greens |
| Kiwi fruit, ripe | Green beans |
| Mammee | Kale |
| Mangoes | Kiwi fruit |

| **Create Ethylene Gas** | **Damaged by Ethylene Gas** |
|---|---|
| Mangosteen | Leafy greens |
| Melons | Lettuce |
| Mushrooms | Parsley |
| Nectarines | Peas |
| Okra | Peppers |
| Papayas | Potatoes |
| Passion Fruit | Potted plants |
| Peaches | Romaine |
| Peppers | Squash |
| Persimmons | Sweet potatoes |
| Pineapple | Watercress |
| Plantains | Yams |
| Plums | |
| Prunes | |
| Quinces | |
| Rambutan | |
| Tomatoes | |
| Watermelon | |

## FOOD-SAFE STEP #5

### Keep a Food Thermometer At-the-Ready:

"It's Safe to Bite When the Temperature Is Right!" says Thermy™

Just as a mother can't judge the degree of her child's body temperature by placing her hand on the child's forehead, you can't "eyeball" if the pork, for example, is thoroughly cooked. An appropriate, accurate thermometer is required to confirm in either case.

Buy four thermometers if you don't already own them:

1. An appliance thermometer to measure the temperature of the refrigerator. It must never go above 40 degrees F.
2. An appliance thermometer in your freezer that should always indicate zero degrees F or less.
3. Use an oven thermometer to indicate the temperature accuracy.
4. Have a food thermometer handy to measure temperatures of hamburgers, etc., as you cook them on the stove or at the grill.

Food must never be allowed to stay between 40 degrees F to 140 degrees F. This is the Temperature Danger Zone. Always cook meat, poultry, fish, and other foods to the proper temperature for each.

# Thermy™

Thermy™ is the messenger of a national consumer education campaign
designed to promote the use of food thermometers, developed by the
Food Safety and Inspection Service (FSIS), U.S. Department of Agriculture (USDA).

Food Safety and Inspection Service, USDA

The USDA owns the copyright and
trademark to Thermy™ art. USDA/FSIS
allows and encourages reproduction of the
Thermy™ art and materials but only for
educational purposes without further
permission. Permission for any other
reproduction and use of Thermy™ must
be granted, depending upon the specific
use, by the USDA/FSIS, Food Safety
Education Staff. (202) 720-7943.

USDA does not endorse any products,
services, or organizations.

www.fsis.usda.gov/thermy

### Executive Chef Robert J. Chantos

I wish the home cook could realize how important temperature is in preventing foodborne illnesses. A calibrated thermometer is one of the most
important tools in a home kitchen. As Thermy™ says: 'Use a food thermometer: It's the only way to tell if your food has reached a high enough
temperature to destroy harmful bacteria.' Cooking food to the proper temperature kills bacteria that cause foodborne illness and death.

While it is important to notice tangible signs of doneness, such as aroma,
appearance, radiation of heat, the best and only true sign of doneness is the core

temperature of the food. Each time the thermometer is inserted in food, use an alcohol wipe or soap and water to clean it; never use an abrasive or caustic compound. The readout device may be cleaned with a damp cloth or paper towel. The probe should be rinsed to remove any residual sanitizer prior to insertion into the food.

Always use a food thermometer to measure the proper internal temperatures:

Ground Meat Products:
    Beef, veal, lamb, pork          160 degrees F

Beef, Veal, Lamb
    Roasts and steaks
        Medium-rare          145 degrees F
        Medium          160 degrees F
        Well-done          170 degrees F

Pork
    Chops, roast, ribs
        Medium          160 degrees F
        Well-done          170 degrees F

Poultry
    Chicken, whole and pieces          180 degrees F
    Ground chicken or turkey          165 degrees F
    Duck          180 degrees F
    Turkey (stuffed, unstuffed)
        Whole          180 degrees F
        Breast          170 degrees F
        Dark meat          180 degrees F
        Stuffing (cooked alone)          165 degrees F

Eggs
    Fried, poached          firm white and yolk
    Casseroles          165 degrees F
    Sauces, custards          160 degrees F

Seafood
    Fillets and whole fish          145 degrees F
    Shellfish          145 degrees F

Look for visual signs that cooked food is safe:

- Food is steaming hot.
- Seafood is opaque; fish flakes easily.

- Egg yolks are firm and not runny: never serve "sunny-side up" again!
- Egg whites are firm with no clear, uncooked, "skin."

---

When using heat as you cook and bake, consider substituting parchment paper or glass baking dishes for aluminum foil and plastic wrap and plastic containers to keep heavy metals and toxic gases out of your food.

---

## FOOD-SAFE STEP #6

### Avoid Cross-Contamination:

Keep It Straight! Separate. Don't Cross-Contaminate!

Definition: Cross-contamination, a leading cause of foodborne illness, is a term that means the transfer of harmful substances or disease-causing microorganisms from one food to another food by hands, food-contact surfaces, sponges, cloth towels or utensils that touch raw food and then handle ready-to-eat foods. Cross-contamination can also occur when raw food touches or drips onto cooked or ready-to-eat foods.

#### Examples of Cross-Contamination at Work

*Ban* unsanitary sponges and dishrags from your kitchen. Use paper towels to wipe up all uncooked or rare poultry meat and fish juices. If using disposable gloves (because of sores or cuts on hands), always wash hands first and dry thoroughly with a disposable paper towel before putting on gloves. Change gloves each time you complete a food preparation task, washing hands again before putting on a fresh pair of gloves.

When preparing fruits and vegetables, cut away any damaged or bruised areas because bacteria that cause illness can thrive in those places. Don't use marinades from raw meat on produce that will not be cooked thoroughly. Always keep raw animal foods separate from cooked and ready-to-eat foods.

---

**Ripped from the News**

In the summer of 2002, a small child died of salmonella after eating a piece of fruit. In order to cut the cantaloupe in two, the fruit was placed on the cutting board that had been used to cut raw meat and had not been cleaned and sanitized. The knife came into contact with the contaminated rind and spread to the inside of the cantaloupe.

Most recipes tell you to rinse the inside and outside of raw poultry. They fail to add that it is then vital to wash and sanitize the sink, counters: *All areas touched by any raw meat, poultry, or fish must be washed and sanitized.*

*Separate* raw meat, poultry, and seafood from other foods from the time of purchase—to storing—to cutting board—to the stove. In this way, you reduce the risk of bacteria transfer during meal preparation and avoid cross-contamination. In the refrigerator, raw meat must be handled very carefully. Do *not* use the same container to store both raw and cooked foods. Be sure no raw meat and poultry are on the same plate, and do not drip on food below in the refrigerator.

Never permit salads or other ready-to-eat products to be prepared on the same surface as raw, uncooked meats: fish, seafood, turkey, pork, beef. Always make sure both the knife and cutting board have been cleaned and sanitized before using them. Then wash and sanitize both after each task. The cutting board may be cleaned by putting in dishwasher, or cleaned and sanitized with one teaspoon of household bleach to one quart of water.

NEW in Culinary Fashions: the very newest sight in the professional kitchens is color! One company has realized that color is the perfect language to communicate food safety. So they have come up with not just cutting boards in these six colors, but with scrapers to take the product from the boards and brushes to clean each board. They offer also colored handles for knives, tongs, forks, steels, spatulas, and turners (see box below).

## FOOD-SAFE STEP #7

### Serving Food the Food-Safe Way:

Keep Cold Foods Cold (40 degrees F or below); Keep Hot Foods Hot (140 degrees F or above).

*Note:* Freezing will not kill foodborne illnesses. Cooking to the proper temperature is the only way to prevent foodborne illnesses.

Always keep a calibrated food thermometer handy and check foods carefully. Cold food must be kept at 40 degrees F or below and hot food at 140 degrees F or above, if food is going to be held before serving.

Before eating hot dogs and luncheon meats, be sure they are kept in the refrigerator so they are cold. When you unwrap both hot dogs and luncheon meats, take time to heat them to 155 degrees F before serving. Allow to cool before serving.

The home cook must realize the importance of following the "Two-Hour Rule": Never leave cooked food out of the refrigerator for more than two hours. Put food away first before serving dessert.

**About Cutting Boards**

If you don't have a cutting board in your kitchen, please buy one or several today. Look at all of the different types that you find on the market.

**Selections:** Check on the way the board interacts with the knife, that it doesn't retain odors or will warp. A large board, not too heavy (maximum 4 pounds) or too bulky, is good as it provides extra work space, but be sure it will fit into your dishwasher. Cutting boards come in hard acrylic, glass, and Corian, which don't absorb the shock of the knife strikes. The softer boards made of wood should be oiled. Plastic is also softer. Boards with feet or to use over the sink may prove wobbly.

**Care:** Wash your cutting board well in the dishwasher after every use. If washing by hand, use hot soapy water followed by a light solution of one tablespoon of *bleach* to a gallon of water.

**New Product:** Cut 'n' Slice Flexible Cutting Mats come in a package of three colors. Each easy-to-clean, lightweight, dishwasher safe mat is 11.5 × 15″. Use on a flat surface, smooth-side up as you chop, grate, peel, slice, and dice. Add a few drops of water to underside of board to prevent slipping. Can be picked up and folded in order to pour cut food item right from mat. (Under $3.00 for set.)

If you cook a lot, you might find it easier to keep items separated by using colored cutting boards as many chefs do:

Red. . .     for raw meats

Yellow. . .     for raw poultry

Blue. . .     for fish

Green. . .     for cutting and chopping fruits and vegetables

White. . .     for dairy products

Brown. . .     for cooked food

In this way, you reduce the risk of transferring bacteria during meal preparation and also avoiding cross-contamination, a leading cause of foodborne illness.

The Centers for Disease Control and Prevention links eating undercooked meat, poultry, and eggs with a higher risk of illness. Therefore, we warn that if a thermometer is not available, *do not eat!*

It can't be repeated enough: clean surfaces, utensils, and hands after touching any raw meat and poultry and before you put fresh produce on these surfaces, on utensils, or touch them with your hands.

A WARNING: **EACH BOARD** MUST BE CLEANED & SANITIZED AFTER **EACH USE.**

---

**Chefs' Best Time-Saving Tip:**

*Mise en place* is a French term used by fine chefs, meaning to prepare, and have ready to combine, all of the ingredients that are necessary to make a dish. Measure out all of the dry and wet ingredients and put each item in its separate small bowl or cup. Then when you are ready to put the recipe together, it will take a much shorter time. Try it! You'll find you'll save time.

---

## FOOD-SAFE STEP #8

### Leftovers Can Be Dangerous:

When in Doubt—Throw It Out!

Wash hands with hot, soapy water before and after handling leftovers, and always use clean plates and utensils.

Refrigerate leftovers quickly—**within two hours**—after serving. The larger the quantity of hot food, the longer it will stay hot. Therefore, when storing hot food in the refrigerator to cool, first divide the large quantities of leftovers into smaller portions and place in a shallow pan—even if it takes two or more to store soups, stews, casseroles, etc. The reason for this is that two separate pints of product cool faster in the refrigerator than a single quart container. Leave space around leftover containers in the refrigerator to assure rapid, even cooling.

Cold food that is to kept for more than 24 hours must be properly date-marked.

Freeze any leftovers you won't eat within two days and DATE.

For food quality and safety, reheat foods that have been cooked. Be sure that food is reheated only one time to 165 degrees F. Never thaw food at room temperature. Refrigerate or freeze large amounts of hot stews and soups in shallow storage containers to cool faster.

### Executive Chef Robert J. Chantos

Never taste-test leftovers. It could be your last meal! None of us want to waste food, but when food is not properly cooked or stored, it could be unsafe to eat. You are safer tossing it out. Think about this: If you do have food left over after two servings, you either made too much at once, or maybe it wasn't that tasty the first time.

Refrigerate or freeze perishables, prepared foods, and leftovers within two hours. Refrigerate when defrosting leftovers. Cold running water and microwave ovens can also be used to defrost.

Make a habit of dating leftovers so they can be used within a safe time. For serving the second time, reheat it to the approved 165 degrees F. before

# PART TWO

# Educational Information

# The Germs: Their Names, Type and Cause of Illness, Common Foods Affected, and the Prevention

**Biological Hazards Include Bacteria, Viruses, and Parasites**
Permission from Prentice Hall to use this information is gratefully acknowledged.

### Foodborne Illnesses Caused by Bacteria

| Causative Agent (* sporeforming bacteria) | Type of Illness | Symptoms Onset | Common Foods or Sources | Prevention |
|---|---|---|---|---|
| * Bacillus cereus | Bacterial intoxication or toxin-mediated infection | 1) Diarrhea type: abdominal cramps (8–16 hours) 2) Vomiting type: vomiting, diarrhea, abdominal cramps (30 min–6 hrs) | 1) Diarrhea type: meats milk vegetables 2) Vomiting type: rice starchy foods grains cereals | Properly heat, cool, and reheat foods |
| * Clostridium perfringens | Bacterial toxin-mediated infection | Intense abdominal pains and severe diarrhea (8–22 hours) | Spices, gravy, improperly cooled foods (especially meats and gravy dishes) | Properly cook, cool, and reheat foods |
| * Clostridium botulinum | Bacterial intoxication | Dizziness, double vision, difficulty in breathing and swallowing, headache (12–36 hours) | Improperly canned foods, vacuum-packed refrigerated foods, cooked foods in anaerobic mass | Properly heat, process anaerobically packed foods; DO NOT use home canned foods |
| Campylobacter jejuni | Bacterial infection | Watery, bloody diarrhea (2–5 days) | Raw chicken, raw milk, raw meat | Properly handle and cook foods; avoid cross contamination |

**Foodborne Illnesses Caused by Bacteria (*cont.*)**

| Causative Agent (* sporeforming bacteria) | Type of Illness | Symptoms Onset | Common Foods or Sources | Prevention |
|---|---|---|---|---|
| *Escherichia coli O157:H7* | Bacterial infection or toxin-mediated infection | Bloody diarrhea followed by kidney failure and hemolytic uremic syndrome (HUS) in severe cases (12–72 hours) | Undercooked hamburger, raw milk, un-pasteurized apple cider, lettuce | Practice good food sanitation, hand washing; properly handle and cook foods |
| *Listeria monocytogenes* | Bacterial infection | 1) Healthy adult: flu-like symptoms 2) At-risk population: septicemia, meningitis, encephalitis, birth defects 3) Still-birth (1 day–3 weeks) | Raw milk, dairy items, raw meats, refrigerated ready-to-eat foods, processed ready-to-eat meats such as hot dogs, raw vegetables, and seafood | Properly store and cook foods; avoid cross contamination; rotate processed refrigerated foods using FIFO to ensure timely use |
| *Salmonella spp.* | Bacterial infection | Nausea, fever, vomiting, abdominal cramps, diarrhea (6–48 hours) | Raw meats, raw poultry, eggs, milk, dairy products | Properly cook foods, avoid cross contamination |
| *Shigella spp.* | Bacterial infection | Bacillary dysentery, diarrhea, fever, abdominal cramps, dehydration (1–7 days) | Foods that are prepared with human contact: salads, raw vegetables, milk, dairy products, raw poultry, non-potable water, ready to eat meat | Wash hands and practice good personal hygiene; properly cook foods |
| *Staphylococcus aureus* | Bacterial intoxication | Nausea, vomiting, abdominal cramps, headaches (2–6 hours) | Foods that are prepared with human contact: cooked or processed foods | Wash hands and practice good personal hygiene: cooking WILL NOT kill the toxin |
| *Vibrio spp.* | Bacterial infection | Headache, fever, chills, diarrhea, vomiting, severe electrolyte loss, gastroenteritis (2–48 hours) | Raw or improperly cooked fish and shellfish | Practice good sanitation; properly cook foods, avoid serving raw seafood |
| *Hepatitis A* | Viral infection | Fever, nausea, vomiting, abdominal pain, fatigue, swelling of the liver, jaundice (15–50 days) | Foods that are prepared with human contact: contaminated water | Wash hands and practice good personal hygiene; avoid raw seafood |
| *Norwalk virus* | Viral infection | Vomiting, diarrhea, abdominal pain, headache, low grade fever; onset 24–28 hours | Sewage, contaminated water, contaminated salad ingredients, | Use potable water, cook all shellfish; handle food properly; meet time, temperature |

**Foodborne Illnesses Caused by Bacteria (*cont.*)**

| Causative Agent (* sporeforming bacteria) | Type of Illness | Symptoms Onset | Common Foods or Sources | Prevention |
|---|---|---|---|---|
| | | | raw clams, oysters, and infected food workers | guidelines for PHF |
| Rotavirus | Viral infection | Diarrhea (especially in infants and children), vomiting, low grade fever; 1–3 days onset; lasts 4–8 days | Sewage, contaminated water, contaminated salad ingredients, raw seafood | Good personal hygiene and hand washing; proper food handling practices |
| Aniskas spp. | Parasitic infection | Coughing, vomiting, onset 1 hour to 2 weeks | Raw or undercooked seafood, especially bottom feeding fish | Cook fish to proper temperature throughout; freeze to meet Food Code specifications |
| Cyclospora cayentanensis | Parasitic infection | Watery and explosive diarrhea, loss of appetite, bloating (1 week) | Water, strawberries, raspberries, and raw vegetables | Good sanitation, reputable supplier |
| Cryptosporidium parvum | Parasitic infection | Severe watery diarrhea within 1 week of ingestion | Contaminated water, food contaminated by infected food handlers | Use potable water supply; practice good personal hygiene and hand washing |
| Giardia lamblia | Parasitic infection | Diarrhea within 1 week of contact | Contaminated water | Potable water supply; good personal hygiene and hand washing |
| Taxoplasma gondii | Parasitic infection | Mild cases of the disease involve swollen lymph glands, fever, headache, and muscle aches. Severe cases may result in damage to the eye or the brain (10–13 days) | Raw meats, raw vegetables, and fruit | Good sanitation, reputable supplier, proper cooking |
| Trichinella spiralis | Parasitic infection from a nematode worm | Nausea, vomiting, diarrhea, sweating, muscle soreness (2–28 days) | Primarily undercooked pork products and wild game meats (bear, walrus) | Cook foods to the proper temperature throughout |
| Ciguatoxin | Fish toxin originating from toxic algae of tropical waters | Vertigo, hot/cold flashes, diarrhea, vomiting (15 min-24 hours) | Marine finfish including grouper, barracuda, snapper, jack, | Purchase fish from a reputable supplier; cooking WILL NOT kill the |

**Foodborne Illnesses Caused by Bacteria (*cont.*)**

| Causative Agent (* sporeforming bacteria) | Type of Illness | Symptoms Onset | Common Foods or Sources | Prevention |
|---|---|---|---|---|
| | | | mackerel, triggerfish, reef fish | toxin |
| Scombrotoxin | Seafood toxin originating from histamine producing bacteria | Dizziness, burning feeling in the mouth, facial rash or hives, peppery taste in mouth, headache, itching, teary eyes, runny nose (1–30 min) | Tuna, mahi-mahi, bluefish, sardines, mackerel, anchovies, amberjack, abalone | Purchase fish from a reputable supplier; store fish at low temperatures to prevent growth of histamine-producing bacteria; toxin IS NOT killed by cooking |
| Shellfish toxins: PSP, DSP, DAP, NSP | Intoxication | Numbness of lips, tongue, arms, legs, neck; lack of muscle coordination (10–60 min) | Contaminated mussels, clams, oysters, scallops | Purchase from a reputable supplier |
| Mycotoxins | Intoxication | 1) Acute onset– hemorrhage, fluid buildup | Moldy grains, corn, corn products, peanuts, pecans, walnuts, and milk | Purchase food from a reputable supplier; keep grains and nuts dry; and protect products from humidity |
| | | 2) Chronic onset– cancer from small doses over time | | |

# That '24-Hour Flu'? It Might Be Something You Ate!

Sometimes it's difficult to determine whether you have the flu or it's a foodborne illness because the symptoms of the flu are very similar to foodborne illness. Here, courtesy of Congra and the American Dietetic Association, is a simple chart to help you:

| Symptoms | "The Flu" | Foodborne Illness |
|---|---|---|
| Aches and pains | Headache, muscle ache | Headache, backache, stomach cramps |
| Fatigue | common | common |
| Fever | common | common |
| Vomiting | rarely prominent | common |
| Diarrhea | rarely prominent | common |
| Coughing | common | rare |
| Sore throat | common | rare |

"There are many things consumers can do to avoid foodborne illness. A little extra hand washing and extra attention to detail when you handle foods or prepare a meal is a small price to pay to proven foodborne illness. We certainly can't guarantee that all the foods that pass our lips at home are completely safe and free of pathogens.

"However, we can wash our hands thoroughly and frequently and take appropriate steps during food shopping, unpacking, and food preparation, and storage to improve our chances of eating safe and delicious food. While 74 percent of those polled know that eating meat not cooked to proper temperatures can cause foodborne illness, only 12 percent use meat thermometers to check doneness."

**Elisa Zied, MS, RD, CDN, a registered dietitian
and certified nutritionist in New York**

# Everything a Home Cook Should Know About Food Thermometers

Courtesy: USDA, Food Safety and Inspection Service, Education Staff

The main thing you need to know about kitchen thermometers is that you should keep four types of thermometers in your kitchen, all in perfect working order: two appliance thermometers, one kept at 40 degrees F in the refrigerator; the other set at −0 degrees F, an oven thermometer; and a food thermometer to keep handy when cooking meat, poultry, and egg products to prevent under-cooking. Each will help to prevent foodborne illnesses.

According to the Food Safety and Inspection Service of the United States Department of Agriculture, one of the critical factors in controlling pathogens in food is controlling temperature. This is how the icon Thermy™ came into being, rising from the fertile brain of Holly Mc Peak, Public Info, USDA.

Disease-causing microorganisms such as bacteria, viruses, and parasites grow very slowly at low temperatures, multiply rapidly in mid-range tempera-tures and are killed at high temperatures. For safety, perishable foods must be held at proper *cold* temperatures to inhibit bacterial growth or *cooked* to temper-atures high enough to kill harmful microorganisms.

## WHY USE A FOOD THERMOMETER?

Using a food thermometer is the only reliable way to ensure safety and to deter-mine the "doneness" of meat, poultry, and egg products. To be safe, these foods must be cooked to an internal temperature high enough to destroy any harmful microorganisms that may be in the food.

"Doneness" refers to when a food is cooked to a desired state and indicates the sensory aspects of foods such as texture, appearance, and juiciness.

## COLOR IS NOT A RELIABLE INDICATOR

Many food handlers believe that visible indicators, such as color changes, can be used to determine if foods are cooked to a point where pathogens are killed. However, recent research has shown that color and texture indicators are unreliable. For example, ground beef may turn brown before it reaches a temperature where pathogens are destroyed. A consumer preparing hamburger patties and using the brown color as an indicator of "doneness" is taking a chance that pathogenic microorganisms may survive. A hamburger cooked to 160 degrees F, regardless of color, is safe.

> "Temperature sensitivity of thermometer probes does not vary by altitude, longitude, or latitude. The only thing that some find confusing is the calibration or validation of these thermometers using boiling water at the high set point. The higher one goes in altitude, the lower is the boiling temperature of water. Therefore, we try to stress that any calibration or validation of a temperature measuring device is done with a temperature-standard thermometer. When this is done, the altitude does not matter—temperature is temperature."
>
> **Dr. Robert Powitz**

## SAFETY VERSUS DONENESS

The temperature at which different pathogenic microorganisms are destroyed varies, as does the "doneness" temperature for different meat and poultry. A roast or steak that is not pierced in any way during processing or preparation and reaches an internal temperature of 145 degrees F is safe to eat. A consumer looking for a visual sign of "doneness" might continue cooking it until it is overcooked and dry. However, a consumer using a food thermometer to check for "doneness" can feel assured the food has reached a safe temperature and is not overcooked.

Likewise, poultry should reach at least 180 degrees F throughout for safety. However, at this temperature, the meat has not reached a traditional "done" texture and color. For this reason, most consumers prefer to cook it longer (to a higher temperature).

A food thermometer should also be used to ensure that cooked foods are held at safe temperatures until served—40 degrees F or below, or 140 degrees F and above.

## TYPES OF THERMOMETERS

Food thermometers come in several types and styles, and vary in level of technology and price.

### Digital Food Thermometers

#### Thermocouples

Of all of the food thermometers, thermocouple thermometers reach and display the final temperature the fastest—within 2 to 5 seconds. The temperature is indicated on a digital display.

A thermocouple measures temperature at the junction of two fine wires located in the tip of the probe. Thermocouples used in scientific laboratories have very thin probes, similar to hypodermic needles, while others may have a thickness of 1/16 of an inch.

Since thermocouple thermometers respond so rapidly, the temperature can be quickly checked in a number of locations to ensure that the food is thoroughly cooked. This is especially useful for cooking large foods, such as roasts or turkeys, when checking the temperature in more than one place is advised. The thin probe of the thermocouple also enables it to accurately read the temperature of thin foods such as hamburger patties, pork chops, and chicken breasts.

Thermocouples are not designed to remain in the food while it's cooking. Instead, they should be used near the end of the estimated cooking time to check for final cooking temperatures. To prevent overcooking, check the temperature before the food is expected to finish cooking. Thermocouples can be calibrated for accuracy.

#### Thermistors

Thermistor-style food thermometers use a resistor (a ceramic semiconductor bonded in the tip with temperature-sensitive epoxy) to measure temperature. The thickness of the probe is approximately 1/8 of an inch and takes roughly 10 seconds to register the temperature on the digital display. Since the semiconductor is in the tip, thermistors can measure temperature in thin foods, as well as thick foods. Because the center of a food is usually cooler than the outer surface, place the tip in the center of the thickest part of the food.

This type of thermometer should be used near the end of the estimated cooking time to check the food. Thermistors are not designed to remain in the food while it's cooking. To prevent overcooking, check the temperature before the food is expected to finish cooking.

Not all thermistors can be calibrated. Check the manufacturer's instructions. If a thermometer can not be calibrated, don't buy it, as any malfunction can lead to inaccuracy.

**Oven Cord Thermometer.** This food thermometer allows the cook to check the temperature of food in the oven without opening the oven door. A base unit with a digital screen is attached to a thermistor-type food thermometer probe by a long metal cord. The probe is inserted into the food, and the cord extends from the oven to the base unit. The base can be placed on the counter or attached to the stovetop or oven door by a magnet. The thermometer is programmed for the desired temperature and beeps when it is reached. While designed for use in ovens, these thermometers can also be used to check foods cooking on the stove.

Oven cord thermometers cannot be calibrated.

**Thermometer Fork Combination.** This utensil combines a cooking fork with a food thermometer. A temperature-sensing device is embedded in one of the tines of the fork. There are several different brands and styles of thermometer forks on the market; some using thermocouples and some using thermistors. The food temperature is indicated on a digital display or by indicator lights on the handle within 2 to 10 seconds (depending on the type). These lights will tell if the food has reached rare, medium, well-done, etc. Particularly useful for grilling, the thermometer fork will accurately measure the internal temperature of even the thinnest foods. The thermometer fork should be used to check the temperature of a food towards the end of the estimated cooking time. Thermometer forks that require batteries are not designed to remain in a food while in the oven or on the grill. Thermometer forks cannot be calibrated.

### Food Thermometers

**Bimetallic-Coil Thermometer.** These thermometers contain a coil in the probe made of two different metals that are bonded together. The two metals have different rates of expansion. The coil, which is connected to the temperature indicator, expands when heated. This food thermometer senses temperature from its tip and up the stem for 2 to 2 1/2 inches. The resulting temperature is an average of the temperatures along the sensing area. These food thermometers have a dial display and are available as "oven-safe" and "instant-read."

**"Oven-Safe" Bimetallic Thermometer.** This food thermometer is designed to remain in the food while it is cooking in the oven, and is generally used for large items such as a roast or turkey. This food thermometer is convenient because it constantly shows the temperature of the food while it is cooking. However, if not left in the food while cooking, they can take as long as 1 to 2 minutes to register the correct temperature.

The bimetal food thermometer can accurately measure the temperature of relatively thick foods (such as beef roasts) or deep foods (foods in a stockpot). Because the temperature-sensing coil on the stem is between 2 to 2 1/2 inches long and the stem is relatively thick, it is not appropriate to measure the temperature of any food less than 3 inches thick.

There is concern that because heat conducts along the stem's metal surface faster than through the food, the area of the food in contact with the thermometer tip will be hotter than the area a short distance to the side (the "potato nail effect"). To remedy this, the temperature should be taken in a second, and even third area, to verify the temperature of the food. Each time the thermometer is inserted into the food, let the thermometer equilibrate (come to temperature) at least 1 minute before reading the temperature. This is difficult to do while the food is cooking on the grill or in the frying pan. Some models can be calibrated. Check the manufacturer's instructions.

**"Instant Read" Bimetallic-Coil Thermometer.**   This food thermometer measures the temperature of a food in about 15 to 20 seconds. It is not designed to remain in the food while it is cooking in the oven but is sold to estimate cooking time for final cooking temperatures. To prevent overcooking, check the temperature before the food is expected to finish cooking.

For accurate temperature measurement, the probe of the bimetallic-coil thermometer must be inserted the full length of the sensing area (usually 2 to 3 inches). If measuring the temperature of a thin food, such as a hamburger patty or boneless chicken breast, the probe should be inserted through the side of the food so that the entire sensing area is positioned through the center of the food. Some models can be calibrated. Check the manufacturer's instructions.

**Single-Use Temperature Indicators.**   One of the most recent developments in the retail food market is the emergence of disposable temperature indicators. Several brands are available, and all make quick work of determining if a food has reached its final temperature. These temperature sensors are designed for specific temperature ranges, for example, 160 to 170 degrees F. It is important that the sensors be used only with foods for which they are intended. Read the package directions to ensure that the temperature the sensor will reach is consistent with the safe temperatures listed in this publication.

The sensors are made from special temperature-sensitive materials. The sensor is inserted into a food. When the food reaches the proper temperature, the sensor changes color. They are designed to be used only once. However, if the desired temperature has not been reached, they can be reinserted until the temperature is reached. These sensors cannot be left in a food while it cooking. They should be used near the end of the estimated cooking time. To prevent overcooking, check the temperature before the food is expected to finish cooking. Disposable temperature indicators are made from materials approved by the FDA for contact with food.

**Pop-up Timers.**   Commonly used in turkeys and roasting chickens since 1965, the "pop-up" temperature device is constructed from a food-approved nylon. The inside contains a stainless steel spring and firing material. The firing material is made of an organic salt compound or an alloy of metals commonly used in other thermo-sensing devices. The tip of the stem is imbedded in the firing material until it melts, releasing the stem, which is then "popped up" by means of the spring. This indicates that the food has reached the final temperature for safety and doneness. Pop-up timers are reliable within 1 to 2 degrees F, if accurately placed in a food; however, checking the temperature of other parts of the food with a conventional food thermometer is recommended.

### Other Types of Food Thermometers

**Liquid-Filled Thermometers.**   Also called "spirit-filled" or "liquid in glass" thermometers, these thermometers are the oldest kind of food thermometer used in home kitchens. They have either metal or glass stems. As the internal temperature of the food increases, the colored liquid inside the stem expands and rises to indicate the temperature on a scale. Heat conduction in the metal stems can cause false high readings. They are designed to remain in the food while it is cooking. They should be inserted at least 2 inches deep into the thickest part of the food, and are, therefore, not appropriate for thin foods. Some liquid-filled thermometers can be calibrated by carefully moving the glass stem within the holder.

**Candy/Jelly/Deep Fry Thermometers.**   These thermometers will measure temperatures ranging from 100 to 400 degrees F. They are used to measure the extra-high temperatures required of candy and jelly making, as well as frying with hot oil.

## Appliance Thermometers

### Refrigerator/Freezer Thermometers

For safety, it is important to verify the temperature of refrigerators and freezers. Refrigerators should maintain a temperature no higher than 40 degrees F. Frozen food will hold its top quality for the longest possible time when the freezer maintains 0 degrees F. An appliance thermometer can be kept in the refrigerator and freezer to monitor the temperature. This can be critical in the event of a power outage. When the power goes back on, if the refrigerator is 40 degrees F or colder, and the freezer is still colder than 40 degrees F, the food is safe. These bimetallic-coil thermometers are specially designed to provide accuracy at cold temperatures.

### Oven Thermometer

An oven thermometer can be left in the oven to verify that the oven is heating to the desired temperatures. These bimetallic-coil thermometers can measure temperatures from 100 to 600 degrees F.

**Food Thermometers**

| Types | Speed | Placement | Usage Considerations |
|---|---|---|---|
| **Digital Thermometers** | | | |
| Thermocouple | 2–5 seconds | 1/4-inch or deeper in the food, as needed | Gives fastest reading<br>Good for measuring temperatures of thick and thin foods<br>Not designed to remain in food while it's cooking<br>Check internal temperature of food near the end of cooking time<br>Can be calibrated<br>More costly; may be difficult for consumers to find in stores |
| Thermistor | 10 seconds | At least 1/2-inch deep in the food | Gives fast reading<br>Can measure temperature in thin and thick foods<br>Not designed to remain in food while it's cooking<br>Check internal temperature of food near the end of cooking time<br>Some models can be calibrated; check manufacturer's instructions<br>Available in "kitchen" stores |
| Oven Cord Thermometer | 10 seconds | At least 1/2-inch deep in the food | Can be used in most foods<br>Can also be used outside the oven<br>Designed to remain in the food while it is cooking in oven or in covered pot<br>Base unit sits on stovetop or counter<br>Cannot be calibrated |
| Thermometer Fork Combination | 2–10 seconds | At least 1/4-inch in the thickest part of food | Can be used in most foods<br>Not designed to remain in food while it is cooking<br>Sensor in tine of fork must be fully inserted<br>Check internal temperature of food near the end of cooking time<br>Cannot be calibrated<br>Convenient for grilling |
| **Dial Thermometers** | | | |
| Oven-Safe, Bimetal | 1–2 minutes | 2–2 1/2 inches deep in the thickest part of the food | Can be used in roasts, casseroles, and soups<br>Not appropriate for thin foods<br>Can remain in food while it's cooking<br>Heat conduction of metal stem can cause false high reading<br>Some models can be calibrated; |

**Food Thermometers (*cont.*)**

| Types | Speed | Placement | Usage Considerations |
|---|---|---|---|
| | | | check manufacturer's instructions |
| Instant-Read, Bimetal | 15–20 seconds | 2–2 1/2 inches deep in the thickest part of the food | Can be used in roasts, casseroles, and soups<br>Temperature is averaged along probe, from tip to 2–3" up the stem<br>Cannot measure thin foods unless inserted sideways<br>Not designed to remain in food while it is cooking<br>Use to check the internal temperature of a food at the end of cooking time<br>Some models can be calibrated; check manufacturer's instructions<br>Readily available in stores |
| **Other** | | | |
| Single-Use Temperature Sensors | 5–10 seconds | Approx. 1/2-inch deep (follow manufacturer's directions) | Designed to be used only once<br>Designed for specific temperature ranges<br>Should only be used with food for which they are intended<br>Temperature-sensitive material changes color when the desired temperature is reached |
| Liquid-Filled (glass or metal stem) | 1–2 minutes | At least 2 inches deep in the thickest part of the food | Used in roasts, casseroles, and soups<br>Can remain in food while it's cooking<br>Cannot measure thin foods<br>Some can be calibrated; check manufacturer's instructions<br>Possible breakage of glass stem while in food<br>Heat conduction of metal stem can cause false high reading |

## DONENESS AND SAFETY

Most pathogens are destroyed between 140 and 160 degrees F. However, for best quality, meat and poultry require various temperatures for "doneness."

## USING THE FOOD THERMOMETER

Most available food thermometers will give an accurate reading within 2 to 4 degrees F. Reading will only be correct, however, if the thermometer is placed in the proper location in the food. If not inserted correctly, or if the food ther-

**Recommended Internal Temperatures***

| Food | F |
|---|---|
| **Ground Meat & Meat Mixtures** | |
| Beef, Pork, Veal, Lamb | 160 |
| Turkey, Chicken | 165 |
| **Fresh Beef, Veal, Lamb** | |
| Medium Rare | 145 |
| Medium | 160 |
| Well-Done | 170 |
| **Poultry** | |
| Chicken & Turkey, Whole | 180 |
| Poultry breasts, roast | 170 |
| Poultry thighs, wings | 180 |
| Duck & Goose | 180 |
| Stuffing (cooked alone or in bird) | 165 |
| **Fresh Pork** | |
| Medium | 160 |
| Well-Done | 170 |
| **Ham** | |
| Fresh (raw) | 160 |
| Precooked (to reheat) | 140 |
| **Eggs & Egg Dishes** | |
| Eggs | Cook until yolk and white are firm |
| Egg Dishes | 160 |
| Leftovers & Casseroles | 165 |

*"All temperatures given in this book are correct and current with USDA's recommended internal temperatures for consumer use." Diane Van Loukhuyzen, USDA Meat and Poultry Hotline for consumers—1-800-535-4555.
Note: These temperatures are not intended for processing, institutional, or food service preparation. Food service professionals should consult their state or local food code.

mometer is placed in the wrong area, the reading will not accurately reflect the internal temperature of the food. In general, the food thermometer should be placed in the thickest part of the food, away from bone, fat, or gristle.

## Check Manufacturer's Instructions

Before using a food thermometer, read the manufacturer's instructions first. The instructions should tell how far the thermometer must be inserted in a food to give an accurate reading. If instructions are not available, check the stem of the food thermometer for an indentation, or "dimple." This shows one end of the location of the sensing device. Dial thermometers must penetrate about 2 to 3 inches into the food. Most digital thermometers will read the temperature in a small area of the tip.

## Where To Place the Food Thermometer

### Meat

When taking the temperature of beef, pork, or lamb roasts, the food thermometer should be placed midway in the roast, avoiding the bone. When cooking hamburgers, steaks, or chops, insert a thermistor or thermocouple in the thickest part, away from bone, fat, or gristle. If using a dial bimetal thermometer, read "thin foods" below.

When the food being cooked is irregularly shaped, such as with a beef roast, check the temperature in several places.

### Poultry

When cooking whole poultry, the food thermometer should be inserted into the thickest part of the thigh (avoiding the bone). If stuffed, the center of the stuffing should be checked after the thigh reads 180 degrees F (stuffing must reach 165 degrees F). If cooking poultry parts, insert food thermometer into the thickest area, avoiding the bone. The food thermometer may be inserted sideways if necessary. When the food is irregularly shaped, the temperature should be checked in several places.

### Thin Foods

When measuring the temperature of a thin food, such as hamburger patty, pork chop, or chicken breast, a thermistor or thermocouple food thermometer should be used, if possible. However, if using an "instant-read" dial bimetallic-coil food thermometer, the probe must be inserted in the side of the food so that entire sensing area (usually 2 to 3 inches) is positioned through the center of the food.

To avoid burning fingers, it may be helpful to remove the food from the heat source (if cooking on a grill or in a frying pan) and insert the food thermometer sideways after placing the item on a clean spatula or plate.

### Combination Dishes

For casseroles and other combination dishes, place the food thermometer into the thickest portion of the food or the center of the dish. Egg dishes and dishes containing ground meat and poultry should be checked in several places.

## Thermometer Care

As with any cooking utensil, food thermometers should be washed with hot soapy water. Most thermometers should not be immersed in water. Wash carefully by hand. Extra care should be taken when probing multiple foods, especially when probing under-cooked meat and poultry.

Use caution when using a food thermometer. Some models have plastic faces, which can melt if placed too close to heat or dropped in hot liquid. Thermometer probes are sharp and should be stored with the probe in the stem sheath. Some glass thermometers are sensitive to rough handling and should be stored in their packaging for extra protection or in a location where they will not be jostled.

## Calibrating a Thermometer

If you want to go to the trouble, there are two ways to check the accuracy of a food thermometer. One method uses ice water, the other uses boiling water. Many food thermometers have a calibration nut under the dial that can be adjusted. Check the package for instructions.

### Ice Water

To use the ice-water method, fill a large glass with finely crushed ice. Add clean tap water to the top of the ice and stir well. Immerse the food thermometer stem a minimum of 2 inches into the mixture, touching neither the sides nor the bottom of the glass. Wait a minimum of 30 seconds before adjusting. (For ease in handling, the stem of the food thermometer can be placed through the clip section of the stem sheath and, holding the sheath horizontally, lowered into the water.) Without removing the stem from the ice, hold the adjusting nut under the head of the thermometer with a suitable tool and turn the head so the pointer reads 32 degrees F.

### Boiling Water

To use the boiling water method, bring a pot of clean tap water to a full rolling boil. Immerse the stem of a food thermometer in boiling water a minimum of 2 inches and wait at least 30 seconds. (For ease in handling, the stem of the food thermometer can be placed through the clip section of the stem sheath and, holding the sheath horizontally, lowered into the boiling water.) Without removing the stem from the pan, hold the adjusting nut under the head of the food thermometer with a suitable tool and turn the head so the thermometer reads 212 degrees F.

For true accuracy, distilled water must be used and the atmospheric pressure must be one atmosphere (29.921 inches of mercury). A consumer using tap water in unknown atmospheric conditions would probably not measure water boiling at 212 degrees F. Most likely it would boil at least 2 degrees F, and perhaps as much as 5 degrees F, lower. Remember that water boils at a lower temperature in a high-altitude area. Check with your local Cooperative Extension Service for the exact temperature of boiling water in your area.

Even if the food thermometer cannot be calibrated, it should still be checked for accuracy using either method. Any inaccuracies can be taken into consideration when using the food thermometer, or the food thermometer should be replaced. For example, water boils at 212 degrees F.

If the food thermometer reads 214 degrees F in boiling water, it is reading 2 degrees too high. Therefore 2 degrees must be subtracted from the temperature displayed when taking a reading in food to find out the true temperature. In another example, for safety, ground beef patties must reach 160 degrees F. If the thermometer is reading 2 degrees too high, 2 degrees would be added to the desired temperature, meaning hamburger patties must be cooked to 162 degrees F.

For Additional Food Safety Information about meat, poultry, or egg products, call the toll-free USDA Meat and Poultry Hotline: 1 (800) 535-4555; (202) 720-3333 (Washington, DC); or 1 (800) 256-7072.

# Label Reading If You Have Food Allergies

A food allergy is an immune system response to a food that the body mistakenly believes is harmful. Once the immune system decides that a particular food is harmful, it creates specific antibodies to it. The next time the individual eats that food the immune system releases massive amounts of chemicals, including histamine, in order to protect the body. These chemicals trigger a cascade of allergic symptoms that can affect the respiratory system, gastrointestinal tract, skin, or cardiovascular system. Scientists estimate that between 6 and 7 million Americans suffer from true food allergies. At the present time, there is no cure for food allergy. Avoidance is the only way to prevent an allergic reaction.

> Anaphylaxis is a severe systemic allergic reaction characterized by hives, swelling, difficulty breathing, wheezing, and gastro-intestinal symptoms.

Although an individual could be allergic to any food, such as fruits, vegetables, and meats, they are not as common as the following eight foods, which account for 90 percent of all food-allergic reactions:

Courtesy: Food Allergy & Anaphylaxis Network (FAAN), a national nonprofit consumer advocacy group, with more than 25,000 members, is based in Virginia. FAAN is dedicated to raise public awareness, to provide advocacy and education, and to advance research on behalf of all those affected by food allergies and anaphylaxis. FAAN may be contacted toll free at (800) 929-4040 to order one or all of the How To Read A Label ($2.00 each) as well as all other information listed here.

Milk                          Fish

Egg                           Shellfish

Peanut                        Soy

Tree nut                      Wheat
   (walnut, cashew, etc.)

Bake for your family without using milk, eggs, or wheat in a recipe and how to make a soy-free stir-fry and at the end of this information, you will find booklets that can be ordered free from FAAN.


## MANAGING A MILK ALLERGY

### Baking

Fortunately, milk is one of the easiest ingredients to substitute in baking and cooking. It can be substituted, in equal amounts, with water or fruit juice. (For example, substitute 1 cup milk with 1 cup water.)

Check all labels carefully. For example, some brands of canned tuna fish contain casein, a milk protein. Many nondairy products contain casein (a milk derivative), listed on the ingredient labels.

The Jewish community uses a system of product markings to indicate whether a food is kosher, or in accordance with Jewish dietary rules. There are two kosher symbols that can be helpful for those with a milk allergy: a "D," or the word dairy, on a label next to "K" or "U" (usually found near the product name) indicates presence of milk protein, and a "DE" on a label indicates produced on equipment shared with dairy.

If the product contains neither meat nor dairy products it is Pareve (Parev, Parve). Pareve-labeled products indicate that the products are considered milk-free according to religious specifications. Be aware that under Jewish law, a food product may be considered Pareve even if it contains a very small amount of milk. Therefore, a product labeled as Pareve could potentially have enough milk protein in it to cause a reaction in a milk-allergic individual.

Be aware: The machine that slices deli meat is frequently used to slice both meat and cheese products.

When eating out: Many restaurants put butter on steaks after they have been grilled to add extra flavor. Although butter is classified as a fat, there are milk solids in it unless it has been clarified.

### Commonly Asked Questions

Is goat milk a safe alternative to cow milk? Goat's milk protein is similar to cow's milk protein and may, therefore, cause a reaction in milk-allergic individuals. It is not a safe alternative.

None of the following ingredients contain milk protein and need not be restricted by someone avoiding milk:

| | |
|---|---|
| Calcium lactate | Lactic acid |
| Cocoa butter | Sodium lactate |
| Cream of tartar | Sodium stearoyl lactylate |
| Calcium stearoyl lactylate oleoresin | |

## MANAGING AN EGG ALLERGY

### Baking

For each egg, substitute one of the following in recipes:

1 tsp. baking powder, 1 T. liquid, 1 T. vinegar

1 tsp. yeast dissolved in 1/4 cup warm water

1/2 T. water, 1/2 T. oil, 1 tsp. baking powder

1 packet gelatin, 2 T. warm water

Do not mix until ready to use. These substitutes work well when baking from scratch and substituting 1 to 3 eggs.

### Some Hidden Sources of Egg

Eggs have been used to create the foam or milk topping on specialty coffee drinks and are used in some bar drinks. Some commercial brands of egg substitutes contain egg whites. Most commercially processed cooked pastas (including those used in prepared foods such as soup) contain egg or are processed on equipment shared with egg-containing pastas. Boxed, dry pastas are usually egg-free. Fresh pasta is usually egg-free, too. Read the label or ask about ingredients before eating pasta.

### Commonly Asked Questions

- Is a flu shot safe for an individual with an egg allergy? Influenza vaccines are grown on egg embryos and may contain a small amount of egg protein. If you or your child is allergic to eggs, speak to your doctor before receiving a flu shot.
- Can an MMR (measles, mumps, and rubella) vaccine be given to an individual with an egg allergy? The recommendations of the American Academy of Pediatrics (AAP) acknowledge that the MMR vaccine can be safely administered to all patients with egg allergy. The AAP recommendations have been based, in part, on overwhelming scientific evidence supporting the routine use of one-dose administration of the MMR vaccine to egg-allergic pa-

tients. This includes those patients with a history of severe, generalized ana-
phylactic reactions to egg.

## MANAGING A PEANUT ALLERGY

### Some Hidden Sources of Peanuts

Artificial nuts can be peanuts that have been deflavored and reflavored with a nut,
such as pecan or walnut. Mandelonas are peanuts soaked in almond flavoring.
Arachis oil is peanut oil. It is advised that peanut-allergic patients avoid chocolate
candies unless they are absolutely certain there is no risk of cross-contact during
manufacturing procedures. African, Chinese, Indonesian, Mexican, Thai, and
Vietnamese dishes often contain peanuts, or are contaminated with peanuts during
preparation of these types of meals. Additionally, foods sold in bakeries and ice
cream shops are often in contact with peanuts. It is recommended that peanut-allergic individuals avoid these types of foods and restaurants. Many brands of sun-
flower seeds are produced on equipment shared with peanuts.

### Keep in Mind

Most experts recommend peanut-allergic patients avoid tree nuts. Peanuts can
be found in many foods. Check all labels carefully. Contact the manufacturer if
you have questions.

   Peanuts can cause severe allergic reactions. If prescribed, carry epinephrine at all times.

### Commonly Asked Questions

- Can a peanut allergy be outgrown? Although once considered to be a life-
  long allergy, recent studies indicate that up to 20 percent of children diagnosed with peanut allergy outgrow it.
- Can alternative nut butters (e.g., cashew nut butter) be substituted for
  peanut butter? Many nut butters are produced on equipment used to
  process peanut butter, therefore making it a somewhat risky alternative.
  Additionally, most experts recommend peanut-allergic patients avoid tree
  nuts as well.

## MANAGING A TREE NUT ALLERGY

### Some Hidden Sources of Tree Nuts

Artificial nuts can be peanuts that have been deflavored and reflavored with a
nut, such as pecan or walnut. Mandelonas are peanuts soaked in almond flavoring. Mortadella may contain pistachios. Natural and artificial flavoring may

contain tree nuts. Tree nuts have been used in many foods including barbecue sauce, cereals, crackers, and ice cream. Kick sacks or hacky sacks, bean bags, and "draftdodgers" are sometimes filled with crushed nut shells.

## Commonly Asked Questions

- Should coconut be avoided by someone with a tree nut allergy? A coconut is the seed of a drupaceous fruit. Coconuts are not typically restricted in the diet of an individual allergic to tree nuts. Some people have reacted to coconut; therefore, discuss this with a doctor before introducing coconut to your diet.
- Is nutmeg safe? Nutmeg is obtained from the seeds of the tropical tree species *Myristica fragrans*. It is safe for an individual with a tree nut allergy.

## Keep in Mind

Tree nuts can cause severe allergic reactions. If your doctor has prescribed epinephrine, be sure to always carry it with you. Most experts advise tree nut-allergic patients to avoid peanuts as well. And, most experts advise patients who have been diagnosed with an allergy to specific tree nuts to avoid all tree nuts.

## MANAGING A FISH AND/OR SHELLFISH ALLERGY

Allergic reactions to fish and shellfish are commonly reported in both adults and children. It is generally recommended that individuals who have had an allergic reaction to one species of fish or positive skin tests to fish avoid all fish. The same rule applies to shellfish. If you have a fish allergy but would like to have fish in your diet, speak with your allergist about the possibility of being challenged with various types of fish.

### Keep in Mind

Fish-allergic individuals should be cautious when eating away from home. They should avoid fish and seafood restaurants because of the risk of contamination in the food-preparation area of their "non-fish" meal from a counter, spatula, cooking oil, fryer, or grill exposed to fish. In addition, fish protein can become airborne during cooking and cause an allergic reaction. Some individuals have had reactions from walking through a fish market. Allergic reactions to fish and shellfish can be severe and are often a cause of anaphylaxis.

## Some Hidden Sources of Fish

Caponata, a traditional sweet-and-sour Sicilian relish, can contain anchovies. Caesar salad dressings and often steak or Worcestershire sauce always contains anchovies. Surimi (imitation crabmeat) often contains fish.

## Commonly Asked Questions

- Should carrageenan be avoided by a fish- or shellfish-allergic individual? Carrageenan, or Irish moss, is a red marine algae, not a fish. This food product is used in a wide variety of foods, particularly dairy foods, as an emulsifier, stabilizer, and thickener. It appears safe for most individuals with food allergies. Carrageenan, since not related to fish or shellfish, does not need to be avoided by those with food allergies.
- Should iodine be avoided by a fish- or shellfish-allergic individual? Allergy to iodine, allergy to radio contrast material (used in some lab procedures), and allergy to fish or shellfish are not related. If you have an allergy to fish or shellfish, you do not need to worry about cross reactions with radio contrast material or iodine.

## MANAGING A SOY ALLERGY

Soybeans have become a major part of processed food products in the United States. Avoiding products made with soybeans can be difficult. Soybeans alone are not a major food in the diet, but because they're in so many products, eliminating all those foods can result in an unbalanced diet. Consult with a dietitian to help you plan for proper nutrition.

## Keep in Mind

Soybeans and soy products are found in baked goods, canned tuna, cereals, crackers, infant formulas, sauces, and soups. At least one brand of peanut butter lists soy on the label. Studies show soy lecithin and soybean oil can be tolerated by most soy-allergic individuals.

Soy-free stir-fry recipe for Stir-Fried Orange Beef: 1 tsp. cornstarch, 1 cup orange juice, 1 to 1-1/2 lb. trimmed beef, thinly sliced, 1 to 2 T. of oil, 1/4 to 1/2 tsp. crushed red pepper flakes, 1 clove minced garlic, 1 T. grated fresh gingerroot, 1/4 cup green onion thinly sliced, 1/4 cup bell pepper thinly sliced. In small bowl, combine cornstarch and orange juice. Set aside. In wok, add beef, oil, and red pepper flakes. Stir-fry over high heat until beef is browned. Remove beef with slotted spoon. Set aside. Add garlic, gingerroot, onion, and bell pepper to oil remaining in the wok.

Stir-fry 2 minutes. Add cornstarch/orange juice mixture. Simmer until thickened. Add beef and toss with sauce. Can be served over noodles or rice.

## MANAGING A WHEAT ALLERGY

### Baking

When baking with wheat-free flours, a combination of flours usually works best. Experiment with different blends to find one that will give you the texture you are trying to achieve. Try substituting 1 cup wheat flour with one of the following:

7/8 cup rice flour

5/8 cup potato starch flour

1 cup soy flour plus 1/4 cup potato starch flour

1 cup corn flour

### Keep in Mind

Read labels carefully. At least one brand of hot dogs and one brand of ice cream contains wheat. It is listed on the label. Many country-style wreaths are decorated with wheat products. Some types of imitation crabmeat contain wheat. Wheat flour is sometimes flavored and shaped to look like beef, pork, and shrimp, especially in Asian dishes, in which it is called Seitan.

## WHAT IS THE DIFFERENCE BETWEEN FOOD ALLERGY AND FOOD INTOLERANCE?

Many people think the terms food allergy and food intolerance mean the same thing; however, they do not. A food intolerance is an adverse food-induced reaction that does not involve the immune system. Lactose intolerance is one example of a food intolerance. A person with lactose intolerance lacks an enzyme that is needed to digest milk sugar. When the person eats milk products, symptoms such as gas, bloating, and abdominal pain may occur.

A food allergy occurs when the immune system reacts to a certain food. The most common form of an immune system reaction occurs when the body creates immunoglobulin E (IgE) antibodies to the food. When these IgE antibodies react with the food, histamine and other chemicals (called mediators) cause hives, asthma, or other symptoms of an allergic reaction.

Here are several general booklets that will help you care for a child or an adult who has allergies.

- *Caring for the Child with Severe Food Allergies* by Lisa Cipriano Collins, MA, MFT. Informative book offers facts and will help families cope with the emotional aspects of raising a severely allergic child. Learn how to reduce risks while encouraging normal emotional development.

- *Food Allergy News Cookbook, Volumes I and II.* Both volumes, packaged in a sturdy, three-ring binder, contain delicious, kitchen-tested recipes, all milk-free. A softcover edition of the *Food Allergy News Cookbook,* containing a compilation of recipes from both Volume I and II, is also available.

- *The Parent's Guide to Food Allergies* by Marianne S. Barber. This book extensively explores all aspects of food allergy management in day-to-day life. A must-have resource for those struggling with a new diagnosis.

There are wallet-sized cards on specific allergies that can be ordered from FAAN for $2.00 each:

**Milk**

- *How to Read a Label for a Milk-Free Diet.* This handy laminated, wallet-sized card lists the synonyms for milk appearing on a label. Great resource to have on your next trip to the grocery store.

- *FAAN Milk Flashback.* The Flashbacks are a great way to read about what has been previously published in *Food Allergy News* that are specific to milk allergy.

**Egg**

- *FAAN Egg Flashback.* The Flashbacks are a great way to read about what has been previously published in the *Food Allergy News* that are specific to egg allergy.

**Peanuts**

- *FAAN Peanut Flashback.* The Flashbacks are a great way to read about what has been previously published in *Food Allergy News* that are specific to peanut allergy.

- *How to Read a Label for a Peanut-Free Diet.* This handy laminated, wallet-sized card lists the ways peanuts can appear on a label. Great resource to take on your next trip to the grocery store.

- *The Peanut Allergy Answer Book* by Michael Young, MD. Comprehensive book covers many topics including anecdotes, research, and more; a great reference tool for those with peanut allergy or anyone who cares for them

**Soy**

- *How to Read a Label for a Soy-Free Diet.* This handy laminated, wallet-sized card lists the synonyms for soy on a label. Great resource to have on your next trip to the grocery store.

- *FAAN Soy Flashback.* The Flashbacks are a great way to read about what has been previously published in *Food Allergy News* that are specific to soy allergy.

**Tree Nuts**

- *How to Read a Label for a Tree Nut-Free Diet.* This handy laminated, wallet-sized card lists the synonyms for tree nuts on a label. Great resource to have on your next trip to the grocery store.
- *FAAN Tree Nut Flashback.* The Flashbacks are a great way to read about what has been previously published in *Food Allergy News* that are specific to tree nut allergy.

**Shellfish**

- *How to Read a Label for a Shellfish-Free Diet.* This handy laminated, wallet-sized card lists the ways shellfish can appear on a label. Great resource to have with you on your next trip to the grocery store.

**Fish**

- *FAAN Fish Flashback.* The Flashbacks are a great way to read about what has been previously published in *Food Allergy News* that are specific to the topic.

# What Is the Difference Between a Food Allergy and a Foodborne Illness?

Many people ask the question of how to tell the difference between a food allergy and a foodborne illness as they become more aware of the symptoms of both a foodborne illness and various allergies.

*Food-Safe Kitchens* covers what foodborne illnesses are and how to prevent them. Actually, the difference between a food allergy and a foodborne illness is that a foodborne illness could affect some people who eat that particular food. However, with a food allergy, a food that may be harmless to one person could produce an allergic reaction in a different person who is allergic to that particular food. With a true food allergy, an individual's immune system will overreact to an ordinarily harmless food. This is caused by an allergic antibody called IgE (*Immunoglobulin E*), which is found in people with allergies.

Now AAAAI gives the full story about allergy, asthma and immunology:

Courtesy of American Academy of Allergy, Asthma, and Immunology, (AAAAI), the largest professional medical specialty organization representing allergists, clinical immunologists, allied health professionals, and other physicians with a special interest in allergy. It was established in 1943 with the merger of the American Association for the Study of Allergy and the Association for the Study of Asthma and Allied Conditions. The mission of the Academy is the advancement of the knowledge and practice of allergy, asthma and immunology.

## WHAT IS THE DIFFERENCE BETWEEN FOOD ALLERGY AND FOOD INTOLERANCE?

Many people think the terms food allergy and food intolerance mean the same thing; however, they do not.

A food allergy occurs when the immune system reacts to a certain food. The most common form of an immune system reaction occurs when the body creates *Immunoglobulin E* (IgE) antibodies to the food. When these IgE antibodies react with the food, histamine and other chemicals (called mediators) cause hives, asthma, or other symptoms of an allergic reaction.

Food allergy often may appear in someone who has family members with allergies, and symptoms may occur after that allergic individual consumes even a tiny amount of the food. Food allergens—those parts of foods that cause allergic reactions—are usually proteins. Most of these allergens can still cause reactions even after they are cooked or have undergone digestion in the intestines. Numerous food proteins have been studied to establish allergen content.

The most common food allergens—responsible for up to 90 percent of all allergic reactions—are the proteins in cow's milk, eggs, peanuts, wheat, soy, fish, shellfish, and tree nuts. The most common allergic skin reaction to a food is hives. Hives are red, very itchy, swollen areas of the skin that may arise suddenly and leave quickly. They often appear in clusters, with new clusters appearing as other areas clear. Hives may occur alone or with other symptoms. Atopic dermatitis, or eczema, a skin condition characterized by itchy, scaly, red skin, can be triggered by food allergy. This reaction is often chronic, occurring in individuals with personal or family histories of allergies or asthma.

Symptoms of asthma, a chronic disease characterized by narrowed airways and difficulty in breathing, may be triggered by food allergy, especially in infants and children. Gastrointestinal symptoms of food allergy include vomiting, diarrhea and abdominal cramping, and sometimes a red rash around the mouth, itching and swelling of the mouth and throat, nausea, abdominal pain, swelling of the stomach and gas.

A food intolerance is an adverse food-induced reaction that does not involve the immune system. Lactose intolerance is one example of a food intolerance. A person with lactose intolerance lacks an enzyme that is needed to digest milk sugar. When the person eats milk products, symptoms such as gas, bloating, and abdominal pain may occur.

Atopic dermatitis, or eczema, a skin condition characterized by itchy, scaly, red skin, can be triggered by food allergy. This reaction is often chronic, occurring in individuals with personal or family histories of allergies or asthma.

Symptoms of asthma, a chronic disease characterized by narrowed airways and difficulty in breathing, may be triggered by food allergy, especially in infants and children.

Gastrointestinal symptoms of food allergy include vomiting, diarrhea, and abdominal cramping, and sometimes a red rash around the mouth, itching and swelling of the mouth and throat, nausea, abdominal pain, swelling of the stomach and gas.

Other symptoms may include feelings of light-headedness, shortness of breath, severe sneezing, anxiety, stomach or uterine cramps, and/or vomiting and diarrhea. In severe cases, patients may experience a drop in blood pressure that results in a loss of consciousness and shock or death could result.

## Anaphylaxis

The first signs of anaphylaxis may be a feeling of warmth, flushing, tingling in the mouth or a red, itchy rash. Other symptoms may include feelings of light-headedness, shortness of breath, severe sneezing, anxiety, stomach or uterine cramps, and/or vomiting and diarrhea. In severe cases, patients may experience a drop in blood pressure that results in a loss of consciousness and shock.

In severe cases, consuming a food to which one is allergic can cause a life-threatening reaction called anaphylaxis, a systemic allergic reaction that can be severe and sometimes fatal.

## Summing Up

Individuals with food allergies will get sick just by eating that type of food. Whereas individuals subject to foodborne illness get sick because there is a breakdown in a critical control point, which allows potentially hazardous bacteria grow or have sufficient numbers to make them ill.

**David Ludwig, Manager,**
**Maricopa Country Environmental Services Dept., Arizona**

# Drinking Raw Juices Is Dangerous

In 1996, three outbreaks of illness in North America were associated with drinking unpasteurized (raw) apple juice. The juice was contaminated with the bacteria *E. coli O157: H7.* In all, 86 people got sick and one child died. Then in 1999, 19 people in Canada became ill after drinking unpasteurized orange juice contaminated with salmonella. Since 1990, there have been at least 14 outbreaks of illness in North America linked to unpasteurized juices, including apple, orange, watermelon, carrot, and coconut juices. **This is a serious problem.**

Does heating used in pasteurization spoil the juice?

- No. Most commercially processed juices are heated to about 185 degrees F for about 16 seconds to destroy yeast and mold. These products are just as nutritious as if they were not heated. And they taste good and last much longer than untreated juice.

Will refrigeration make the juice safe?

- No. Refrigeration does not destroy *E. coli O157: H7* or other bacteria. Refrigeration will slow the growth of germs, bacteria, yeast, and mold in juices, but it will not make or keep unpasteurized juice safe.

What about washing the fruit before you make the juice?

- Washing the fruit before you make juice will reduce the numbers of harmful germs and bacteria on the peel, but it will not remove them all.

Using a weak bleach solution of bleach and water will help when you wash the fruit. Because it takes only a few of these organisms to make you sick (especially if you are at higher risk), washing alone cannot be relied upon to eliminate the risk of getting sick.

Read the label of every juice before you buy so that you won't purchase unpasteurized juice without being aware of it.

# New Education
# for Pregnant Women

If you are expecting a baby, this is a very exciting time in your life. Now it is extremely important that you take the very best care of your body and what you eat. Attention to food safety is especially urgent.

The four associations listed at the bottom of this page have joined together to present information to you that will help you make safe decisions when selecting and preparing food for yourself and your family. Hormonal changes during pregnancy have an effect on the mother's immune system that lead to an increased susceptibility to listeriosis. This foodborne illness can be transmitted to the fetus through the placenta even if the mother is not showing signs of illness. This can result in premature delivery, miscarriage, fetal death, and severe illness or death of a newborn from infection.

Do not eat: Hot dogs, luncheon meats, or deli meats *unless they are reheated to 155 degrees F.*

Persons who are "high risk," such as pregnant women and those with weakened immune systems, are advised not to eat the typical "deli cold cuts," or to thoroughly reheat them before eating. The concern is listeriosis, a serious infection caused by eating foods contaminated with the bacterium *Listeria monocytogenes.* A healthy person may consume food contaminated with the listeria without becoming ill, but pregnant mothers can pass the listeriosis to their

Courtesy of Association of Women's Health, Obstetric and Neonatal Nurses; International Food Information Council Foundation; U.S. Department of Agriculture; and U.S. Department of Health and Human Services.

babies with serious health results. Others with weakened immune systems could get listeriosis after eating food contaminated with even a few bacteria. The bacterium that causes listeriosis is found in both the soil and water. Vegetables could become contaminated, as can uncooked meats and even processed foods that become contaminated after processing (such as the cold cuts at the deli counter).

Listeria is killed by pasteurization, and the heating procedures used to prepare the deli cold cuts should be sufficient to kill the bacterium. However, unless good manufacturing processes are followed, contamination can occur after processing. Unpasteurized milk, or the cheeses made from it, may also contain listeria.

Prevent listeriosis by thoroughly cooking raw food from animal sources. Wash raw vegetables thoroughly before eating. Keep uncooked meats separate from vegetables and from cooked or ready-to-eat foods. Avoid cheeses made from unpasteurized milk. These are usually imported soft cheeses.

Persons at high risk should avoid all soft cheeses (such as feta, brie, Camembert, and Mexican-style cheese, refrigerated pate, or meat spreads).

Also avoid refrigerated smoked seafood unless it is an ingredient in a cooked dish such as a casserole (examples of refrigerated smoked seafood include salmon, trout, whitefish, cod, tuna, and mackerel—mostly labeled "nova-style," "lox," "kippered," "smoked," or "jerky" found in the refrigerated section or sold at deli counters of grocery stores and delicatessens) and foods that contain unpasteurized milk.

**Do not drink:**
> Raw (unpasteurized) milk
> Raw (unpasteurized) juices

**You can safely eat:**
> Hard cheeses
> Semi-soft cheeses such as mozzarella
> Pasteurized processed cheeses slices and spreads
> Cream cheese
> Cottage cheese
> Canned or shelf-stable pate and meat spreads
> Canned fish such as salmon and tuna or shelf-stable smoked seafood

The Food and Drug Administration and the U.S. Department of Agriculture monitor food regularly. When a processed food is found to be contaminated, food monitoring and plant inspection are intensified, and if necessary, the implicated food is recalled.

Keep your food safe from harmful bacteria. Follow the Eight Food-Safe Steps found in the front of *Food-Safe Kitchens.* Wash hands, knives, and cutting boards after handling uncooked foods.

**After baby is born:**

- Take extra attention to hygiene as baby not only has a low resistance, but brings the risk of extra contamination with diapers, bibs, etc.
- Make sure that everything is clean that touches baby.
- Wash your hands after changing baby and before feeding. Make sure that everyone who touches baby does the same.
- Clean the area where baby was changed and keep it dry.
- Separate baby's clean and contaminated materials.

# *Teaching Children Food Safety*

Diane Nelson* says that one of the best ways to teach food safety to children is to practice it yourself—and to be vocal about why it is being practiced. Begin as soon as the child is aware of food and gets beyond throwing it and starts to take interest in all types of food.

- Teach your child about proper hand washing: Talk about all the things hands do—clap, make clay figures, build sand castles, pet animals, and carry food to your mouth. Busy hands must always be washed with soap and water before handling food.
- Let children look at their hands with a magnifying glass. Remind them that dirt and germs can hide in the lines, cracks, and wrinkles. They might see dirt, but they won't see germs as they are too small.
- Let younger children personalize their ideas about germs by tracing their hands or making a fingerprint and then adding eyes, nose, mouth, and hair.
- Show how germs grow: Children can quickly learn that "bad germs make you sick."

This simple demonstration shows how much faster germs grow on a table—or your fingers—than in the refrigerator. You'll need three small dishes and three packets of dry yeast. Put about 1/4 cup boiling water in first dish and

---

*Courtesy, Iowa State University, University Extension, Ames, Iowa, Diane Nelson, extension communication specialist.

1/4 cup room temperature water in the second dish and 1/4 cup ice water with an ice cube in the third. Read the label to see if you need to add sugar to help the yeast grow. In a few minutes you should have dramatic evidence that yeast grows faster at room temperature than at hot or cold temperatures. This is because: (1) you started with billions of live yeast cells, and (2) at the right temperature yeast produces a lot of gas (carbon dioxide) that makes it bubble and rise.

- It can make a lasting impression on a child to see how fast "germs" grow. Most bacteria don't produce gas to bubble and rise and most foods don't have as many bacteria on them as the amount of yeast that we started with. But, it also takes many times fewer bacteria to make us sick.
- Help children practice washing their hands: In the presence of a younger child, remind all of the family members to wash their hands with warm, soapy water before and after handling food and before sitting down to eat a meal.
- If a sink is too high for a child, provide a small stool to stand on. Give the child his or her own roll of paper towels to wipe hands when the washing is done. Give the child his or her own squeeze bottle and let the younger kids decorate a pump dispenser; then fill it with liquid soap.
- The first few times, do a show and tell—explaining how both hands are wet in warm running water, then soap is squeezed into one palm from the child's own bottle. Next, show how hands are rubbed together thoroughly until the lather forms.
- As hands should be washed for a total of at least twenty seconds, sing the song "Happy Birthday." Provide a small soap brush and show how to clean fingernails and between the fingers. The little hands are then rinsed under running water until no more soap remains. Hands are dried on one or two of the paper towels.
- Thermy™ Rules for Kids! If you are old enough to cook, you are old enough to always use a food thermometer when you cook. See how a food thermometer helps make sure this food has reached a high enough temperature to kill harmful bacteria.
- Remember, the color of cooked meat—whether it's pink or brown inside—can fool you. The only way to be sure cooked food is safe to eat is by using a food thermometer. Place the thermometer in the thickest part of most foods, away from any bones and fat.
- Let older children make a chart for their own use giving the safe internal temperatures.

# Seniors' Food-Safe Alert

This Room Is Equipped With

*Edison Electric Light.*

Do not attempt to light with match. Simply turn key on wall by the door.

The use of Electricity for lighting is in no way harmful to health, nor does it affect the soundness of sleep.

Special thanks to the Madsen Electric Museum for the discovery, background and history of this sign.

This was a reassuring sign to the people who lived between 1892 and 1912, but today it makes you smile. It would probably bring a good amount at today's auction.

That was then—when a "stomach upset" was called food poisoning. This is now! Today it's called foodborne illness. As Dr. Robert Tauxe said: "That '24-hour flu'? It might be something you ate!"

It is possible to become sick anytime from 20 minutes to 6 weeks after eating food that wasn't cooked to the proper temperature or had been prepared by someone with unclean hands.

Food today is produced and distributed differently. The food found in your local grocery store comes from all over the world. Science has discovered new and dangerous bacteria in food that was unknown years ago. Food-related illnesses are caused when pathogens enter the food supply.

Seniors must be aware that illness can be caused by harmful bacteria in food. It is difficult for people to recognize when harmful bacteria in food has made them sick because if food is unsafe, you can't see, smell, or taste the bacteria it may contain. These foodborne diseases are currently estimated to cause approximately 76 million illnesses, 325,000 hospitalizations, and 5,200 deaths in the United States each year. The manufacturers, processors, and distributors of food products are making a conscious effort to practice the phrase "Don't break the Cold Chain from the farm to the fork."

However, research indicates that the home cook is unaware of the proper way to handle, prepare, and cook foods in the home kitchen. When the consumers don't know the rules, they can't win the game. For example, as you will note in another chapter about eggs, say goodbye to "Sunny-Side-Up" eggs.

Since one in every 20,000 eggs produced in the United States is estimated to be contaminated with salmonella, the FDA, on September 4, 2001, mandated that shell egg cartons carry safe-handling instructions: To prevent illness from bacteria, keep eggs refrigerated, and cook eggs until yolks are firm. Cook foods containing eggs thoroughly to an internal temperature of 160 degrees F.

In the older age group, you may find your body's ability to fight-off dangerous bacteria that may invade the body through the food we eat is more at-risk for illness, and then, once ill, it seems to take longer to recover. Pathogens and other microorganisms have an effect on bodies of people over 60.

The best preventative is to understand the safeguards necessary to remain free from foodborne illness. Some of the changes seniors undergo lessen the body's ability to combat bacteria. For example, there is a decrease in stomach acid secretion, which is a natural defense against ingested bacteria. And over time, the immune system may become less adept in ridding the body of bacteria.

Too, the sense of taste or smell—sometimes affected by medication or illness—may not always sound an alert when meat is spoiled or milk may be sour. By knowing how the body changes and using safe food-handling techniques, seniors can easily protect themselves and reduce the risk of foodborne illness.

Federal studies show that seniors do a better job of handling food safely than any other age group. But, when it comes to staying safe, you can never know too much. Won't you agree that knowledge of safe food handling is needed to help all age groups stay healthy?

Here, direct from the USDA, are Guidelines for Safe Food Handling:

- Keep it safe, refrigerate or freeze. Refrigerate or freeze all perishable foods. Refrigerator temperature should be 40 degrees F or less; freezer temperature should be 0 degrees F or less. Use a refrigerator/freezer thermometer to check the temperature.

- Never thaw food at room temperature. Always thaw food in the refrigerator, or in cold water or in a microwave. When thawing in the microwave, you must cook the food immediately.

- Wash hands with warm, soapy water before preparing food. Wash hands, utensils, cutting boards, and other work surfaces after contact with raw meat and poultry. This helps prevent cross-contamination.

- Never leave perishable food out of refrigeration over two hours. If room temperature is 90 degrees F or above, food should not be left out over one hour. This would include items such as take-out foods, leftovers from a restaurant meal, and "meals-on-wheels" deliveries.

- Thoroughly cook raw meat, poultry and fish. Do not partially cook food. Have a constant heat source, and always set the oven at 325 degrees F or higher when cooking.

- Do not eat soft cheese such as feta, brie, and camembert cheeses, blue-veined cheeses, and Mexican-style cheeses such as "queso blanco fresco."

- Cheeses that may be eaten include hard cheese; semi-soft cheeses such as mozzarella; pasteurized processed cheeses such as slices and spreads; cream cheese; and cottage cheese. Do not eat refrigerated pates or meat spreads. Canned or shelf-stable pates and meat spreads may be eaten.

- Do not refrigerate smoked seafood, unless it is contained in a cooked dish, such as a casserole. Refrigerated smoked seafood, such as salmon, trout, whitefish, cod, tuna, or mackerel, is most often labeled as "nova-style," "lox," "kippered," "smoked," or "jerky." These fish are found in the refrigerator section or sold at deli counters of grocery stores and delicatessens. Canned or shelf-stable smoked seafood may be eaten.

- Do not drink raw (unpasteurized) milk or eat foods that contain unpasteurized juice.

The U.S. Food and Drug Administration is warning the public about the risks of foodborne illness from eating raw sprouts, because of a recent *E. coli* outbreak associated with alfalfa sprouts. The FDA first warned the public about raw sprouts in 1999. The FDA advised that children, the elderly and people with weak immune systems should not eat raw or lightly cooked sprouts, although raw sprouts have been implicated in illnesses affecting all age groups, stating, "Those persons who wish to reduce their risk of foodborne illness should not eat raw sprouts." For people in high-risk categories, an *E. coli* infection may lead to serious foodborne illness. The FDA advised that people thoroughly cook sprouts before eating. Also, consumers who want to reduce their risk of illness should request that restaurants not add raw sprouts to their food.

To keep food safe from harmful bacteria, follow these four simple steps:

*Clean:* Wash hands and surfaces often.

*Separate:* Don't cross-contaminate.

*Cook:* Cook to proper temperatures.

*Chill:* Refrigerate promptly.

## GOOD ADVICE FOR BOTH CHILDREN AND ADULTS WHO CARE FOR THEIR PETS: USE EXTRA HYGIENE CARE

The presence of any pet in the house increases the risk of cross-contamination. So from the first time a child touches a pet, be sure that children of all ages wash their hands and before preparing food or eating. All pets should be kept out of the kitchen and never be permitted to get up on any kitchen surface. If a cat seems to get up on the counter when alone, be sure, before beginning to prepare a meal, to clean and sanitize the counters.

Whoever empties the cat box should use disposable gloves and hands should be washed thoroughly after discarding the gloves. When there is an animal in the home, the house should be cleaned more often. The presence of pets also causes higher dust and may induce allergen reactions in people who are susceptible.

## WHEN YOU GO OUT TO EAT

You may find a statement on the menu that is there to "disclose" and "remind" consumers that undercooked animal products increase the risk of foodborne illness. This includes raw or undercooked eggs, as well as meat and seafood. Even items like meringue pies might need such a statement. It is a tool for the public to make educated decisions prior to selecting a menu item. Seared tuna is one such item, as is undercooked hamburger or eggs overeasy. It doesn't prohibit the public from ordering it but makes them aware.

# *Do You See What I See?*

You will find after using the easy Eight Food-Safe Steps you have found in this book that you will begin to notice mistakes made during TV food shows, both local and national. Also, look for recipes given in the print media that don't include any of these steps. While you may find some recipes that sound good on television, in newspapers, or in magazines, note that the "experts" rarely suggest testing the food with a thermometer.

While we all love the famous TV chefs, please don't copy their every move. Don't drape the ubiquitous towel over your shoulder, or plunge a finger into the soup to check the temperature, or use the tasting spoon more than once.

Soon you will begin to notice TV commercials that show a breakfast of sunny-side-up eggs or the man at a picnic who takes his fork out of his mouth and uses it to help himself to more food and many more such questionable practices. Or the woman who should know better, putting her tasting spoon in the pan on the stove—twice, or the equally famous woman who always manages to touch her hair while cooking.

If you can find more examples, please let the author know.

# PART THREE

# Happy Holidays
# All Year

# Food-Safe Entertaining

**Chef Robert J. Chantos**

On every occasion: if you have to stop preparing food to greet your guests, don't shake their hands or you will have to rewash before continuing work in the kitchen. If they protest, laugh and say, "It's bad luck to shake the hands of a working chef.

The times when groups of people get together to eat and celebrate could be the most lethal time of the year. Unless you follow the food-safety rules found throughout this book, it is possible that one in every five people at your party could be at special risk from foodborne illness.

Think about your family and guests. Is anyone over 65? Is one of the guests a pregnant woman? Will any younger children attend? Does anyone have a chronic illness?

You can see that there could be a number who are especially vulnerable to foodborne illness. But here's the most important part. You can cut those risks, protecting yourself and your family. The best news: *safe food handling can prevent most foodborne illness.* Remember: "That '24-hour flu'? It might be something you ate!"

Nothing deflates the happiness of a host or hostess who gave a great party last night to have one or more guests call the next day—to say they are in bed with the "flu."

## FOODBORNE INFECTIONS IN THE HOME
## CAN BE LINKED TO SOCIAL FUNCTIONS

According to a recent study, food is the predominant transmitter of infectious intestinal diseases and seems to be linked to social functions such as barbecues and dinner parties. Most frequently reported pathogen was salmonella. Poultry, desserts containing raw eggs, and egg dishes were commonly implicated, with the most common faults in food hygiene being inappropriate storage, inadequate cooking, and cross-contamination.

You know not to handle food when ill. But if you have open cuts and sores on your hands and must prepare a meal for your family, wear a pair of gloves. First, wash your hands carefully and well, dry them on a paper towel, and then put on the gloves.

## INFORMAL PARTIES/BUFFETS

- Remember the "two-hour" rule when entertaining with a large meal or buffet. Don't let perishable foods linger for longer than two hours in the danger zone between 40 degrees F to 140 degrees F.
- Prepare foods quickly, cook them thoroughly, and serve them immediately. Keep hot foods hot with warming trays, chafing dishes or slow cookers that measure at least 140 degrees F. Keep cold foods cold by resting serving dishes on crushed ice.
- Serve small bowls or trays of food and replace them often. Store replacement dishes in the oven or the refrigerator prior to serving.
- It is unsafe to add new food to a serving dish that has been sitting at room temperature for more than two hours. Remove all foods from a buffet after two hours.

### Ice

Most hosts buy ice in quantity for their parties. Consider ice as a food. Contaminated ice can make people sick. Here are guidelines to avoid contamination in ice making: Once the ice is brought home, it must be handled carefully. Wash off the packages with cold water, and then wash your hands before opening the packages. Put the ice in a large clean container with a big scoop to keep guests from putting their hands into the ice.

### Finger Foods

Give each person a separate dish so he or she will be the only one to "finger" that food. Provide proper tools so guests can handle their foods in a safe manner. After all, you can't be sure your guests know when to wash their hands, so prevent guests from "double dipping."

## Fondue Pot

If you are using a fondue pot, or serving cheese balls or strawberries ready to be dipped in chocolate, take what the chefs call "extra prep time." Put the cheese on the crackers and dip the strawberries in advance; station a friend at the fondue pot to scoop out the melted cheese into each guest's small separate bowl and hand out toothpicks. Keep a food thermometer handy to keep the ingredients in the pot at 140 degrees F.

## Be Generous

Put out a big supply of paper plates. Encourage guests to take a fresh plate for each refill and have ample wastebaskets visible. Placing several large forks near the plate of meat and cheese slices and some tablespoons next to the bowl of potato salad will surely give them the idea.

## Silently Help

Hand guests the needed utensil. Inserting a frilly toothpick in each small cube of cheese or vegetable gives a festive air and prevents guests from touching the food. In the area where do-it-yourself sandwiches are to be made, put out a supply of individual plastic knives near the condiments to spread bread or rolls.

Occasionally eggs with clean, uncracked shells can be contaminated with salmonella bacteria, so be careful not to consume raw eggs. You need to take precaution when preparing food made with eggs, especially some desserts like pumpkin or custard pies. Foods like custard, containing eggs, milk, and high-moisture content, need to be cooked to 160 degrees F or until firm. They also must be refrigerated after cooking, a precaution that's not necessary with most cakes, breads, or cookies.

Don't eat raw dough if made with raw eggs! Use commercially pasteurized eggnog or make your own eggnog with a cooked custard base.

Before you begin preparing holiday dishes, remember that clean hands are the key! Always wash hands with warm, soapy water before and after food preparation, as well as when you're handling raw animal products, such as raw eggs.

Beware of cross-contamination. Foodborne illness can occur when kitchen equipment is not thoroughly washed between uses. Always wash surfaces and cooking equipment, including blenders, in hot, soapy water before and after food preparation.

## Cook and Keep Cool

- Bacteria can multiply in moist foods, including desserts and salads containing high-protein foods. Refrigeration slows bacterial growth, so it's important to refrigerate eggs and egg-containing foods as well as meat, poultry and seafood.

- Here, again, the "two-hour rule" is very important to follow: Don't leave perishables out at room temperature for more than *two* hours. Bacteria love to multiply in protein-rich foods.
- Whether you like your breakfast eggs scrambled or fried, always cook eggs until the yolks and whites are firm. Sunny-side-up eggs are a thing of the past for the immune-compromised, especially.
- Tasting is tempting, but licking a spoon or tasting raw cookie dough made with raw eggs from a mixing bowl can be risky. Bacteria could be lurking in the raw eggs.
- Cook cheesecakes, lasagna, baked ziti, and egg dishes to an internal temperature of at least 160 degrees F. Use a food thermometer to check to be sure.

## CONSIDER LEFTOVERS AND STORAGE

- While it is tempting to leave the turkey sitting out for snacking after a meal, you should refrigerate leftovers promptly in covered, shallow containers so they cool quickly.
- Avoid overstocking the refrigerator to allow cool air to circulate freely. Remove turkey from the bone and store separately from stuffing and gravy. Reheat leftovers to at least 165 degrees F.
- Bring gravy to a full, rolling boil and stir during the process. Use leftover turkey and other cooked dishes within two to three days. Use stuffing and gravy within two days.

### Halloween Cider

Unpasteurized apple cider and mulled cider and other drinks made from unpasteurized apple cider are also popular holiday beverages that may contain harmful bacteria. To be sure cider is safe, use ciders labeled as pasteurized, or ensure that you bring unpasteurized cider to a boil before serving. This is especially important for children, the elderly, and people with weakened immune systems.

# Turkey Day Talk

As the legend goes, ever since the Wampanoag Indians helped the settlers celebrate their first harvest with a three-day feast at Plymouth Colony, the turkey has been the focal point at the Thanksgiving table.

Here is the step-by-step process to keep your holiday safe—from purchasing to preparing and roasting in order to control the hazards so that you serve a safe holiday bird.

## PURCHASING THE TURKEY

Whether you thaw the bird or buy fresh, it is important that you do not allow any of the juice to drip on any other foods. *It is highly recommended not to rinse poultry because the pathogens contaminate the sink, the faucet, your hands, and other parts of the kitchen.* (See "Preparing the Bird" below). Rinsing poultry greatly increases the risk of foodborne illness from cross-contamination. The critical step is to get the poultry into the oven to kill the pathogenic bacteria as soon as possible.

## THAWING

- *Never thaw a frozen turkey on the kitchen counter.*
- While the USDA and FDA say that poultry should be thawed in the refrigerator, even in today's colder refrigerators this may take 24 hours for

every 4 to 5 pounds of bird, and the highly contaminated juice from the bird can easily contaminate other foods.

- Poultry should always be thawed on a large platter placed on the bottom refrigerator shelf so that there are minimal chances of cross-contamination. When you believe that the poultry is thawed, make absolutely sure by probing in the middle of the bird to check for any ice. Many foodborne illnesses associated with turkey are caused by the bird not being totally thawed prior to cooking.

- Remember that the critical step in thawing turkey is to make sure the center is thawed and that you take care not to get any juice on kitchen surfaces.

## PREPARING THE BIRD

- Just about every recipe will tell you to rinse the turkey inside and out with fresh running water and pat it dry. Few, except for the Food Safety and Inspection Service, USDA, mention that after the bird is safely in your oven, this is the next most important step: wash the sink, countertops, and your hands with warm, soapy water and then sanitize all areas the bird has touched (not the bird) with a solution of one tablespoon of liquid chlorine bleach per quart of water.

- Actually rinsing any raw poultry, beef, pork, lamb, veal before cooking is not recommended. Cooking the bird to a temperature of 180 degrees F destroys bacteria present on the surface.

Callers to the USDA Meat and Poultry Hotline sometimes ask about soaking poultry in salt water. This is a personal preference. If you choose to do this, prevent cross-contamination by washing all kitchen surfaces and any utensils used with hot soapy water. Do not use kitchen towels that are cloth for hands or other things. Use only paper towels.

- Bacteria in raw juices can spread from one food to another. This is called cross-contamination. Wash hands, cutting boards, dishes, and utensils before handling food such as fruits or vegetables. This is why *Food-Safe Kitchens* stresses that you practice good handwashing before and after handling raw foods as well as any items on the list given in Food-Safe Step #1.

- Never reuse any disposable packing materials such as foam meat trays, egg cartons, or plastic wrap. (Trays and cartons are recyclable.)

## TO STUFF OR NOT TO STUFF

Most food professionals believe it is best not to stuff poultry, but if you insist that you must, it is critical that you never stuff the turkey the day before!

The critical concerns are that the bacteria inside the cavity of the bird will not be destroyed. A stuffed bird takes more time to cook through to the middle. Make the stuffing just before cooking the bird and place the stuffing in the cavity just before putting it in the oven. Cooked giblets may be used in the stuffing *if* they are cooled first.

Julia Child, herself, is against stuffing the bird. "Cook the dressing separately," she advises in *From Julia Child's Kitchen*. She says that an unstuffed turkey is easier to prepare, presents no spoilage problem, and the breast is juicer. Instead, Julia suggests trussing a handful of aromatic vegetables inside the cavity to flavor the meat. Cook the dressing separately, perhaps adding olives and mushrooms to a sausage stuffing.

### Executive Chef Charles Wiley, Elements at the Sanctuary, Phoenix, AZ

As turkeys must be roasted to 160 to 170 degrees F, this could turn the breast to sawdust. In our kitchen, we put vegetables, bay leaf, carrots and onions in the pan and roast the turkey at 300 to 325 degrees F for about three hours with a thermometer in the breast. If the home cook wants to massage it a bit—wrap the breast in foil and roast it very slowly so that the heat penetrates the middle of the leg—it is possible to cook the turkey whole.

## A Stuffed Turkey:

- Use a food thermometer and set the oven temperature at 325 degrees F. The critical temperature and time for cooking the turkey to assure safety is 180 degrees F in the thigh and 165 degrees F in the center of the stuffing.
- Pan-roasting the bird, covered, is the preferred method because it steams and cooks faster and more thoroughly. Then, in the last 45 minutes, uncover the pan and let the turkey brown in the oven. This is a much more assured way to achieve a proper kill of the vegetative bacteria as opposed to cooking the bird uncovered.

## COOKING THE TURKEY FROM THE FROZEN STATE

### A Very Safe Practice

Use the same oven temperature, 325 degrees F. Take off the plastic packaging. Cook the bird in a covered roasting pan. After about 1 1/2 hours in the oven, the bird will be thawed; it will be hot on the outside, so use tongs to handle the bird; you need to remove the giblets, neck, etc. Then, cover the turkey and continue cooking to the end temperature of 180 degrees F in the thigh.

## HOLDING THE TURKEY FOR LATE ARRIVALS

If you plan to hot hold the turkey after cooking, plan to have the turkey done 30 to 60 minutes before you want to serve. If the oven is available, simply turn the control to 200 degrees F. to hot hold. Keep the thermometer in the bird and maintain the temperature above 140 degrees F.

## SERVING THE BIRD

After cooking, take the turkey out of the oven and remove the stuffing (if you've stuffed the bird). Put stuffing on a platter to serve.

Now is the time that your hands must be scrupulously clean. And whoever will carve the turkey must wash his or her hands thoroughly. Using clean, sanitized utensils, carve the turkey meat off the bone. Now it is ready to serve. Serve the stuffing with the turkey.

Beware of **two-hour** limit: It is important to note the time when the turkey is ready to serve. You have just two hours between removing the turkey from the oven and taking the remaining turkey back to the kitchen to put the leftovers into the refrigerator.

Do not package your turkey leftovers in a pile over two inches thick.

## USING THE TURKEY MEAT

- If you have followed the steps above, after the turkey is cooked and served, and promptly stored in the refrigerator, reheating is not a critical control point for safety, and you can safely eat the leftover turkey cold or reheated.
- However, if you have "temperature abused" the turkey by allowing it to sit at room temperature for many hours, reheating will not guarantee the safety of your leftover turkey. Even if it tastes fine, you can become very ill. Illness-caused microorganisms do not normally cause food to smell or taste bad. Remember when it doubt, throw it out!

# Holiday Foods

## MAKING HOLIDAY FOOD GIFTS

During the holidays, people tend to give food gifts when they can't think of anything more appropriate. Here are suggestions for a hectic time.

- If you receive a gift of a bottle of vegetables and herbs in oil, first mark the date on bottle for one week in advance of that day. Then store in the refrigerator after opening, and be sure to discard after one week.
- If you are given a gift of home-prepared food products stored in oil, ask when the product was prepared. Mark the containers with the date a week in advance of the preparation date.
- Commercially prepared products stored in oil that contain an acid (such as vinegar) or salt in their list of ingredients are generally considered to be safe. Store them in the refrigerator after opening and between each use. Contact the manufacturer if there is any doubt about the ingredients in a particular product.
- When making a food gift, always use fresh ingredients to prepare products stored in oil. It is a nice touch to date the bottle with the date the gift was prepared.
- Be sure to handle eggnog and other recipes with eggs safely. Serve cooked eggnog using the directions below or use pasteurized egg products, found in most grocery outlets.
- If you choose to make eggnog with whole eggs, heat the egg-milk mixture to 160 degrees F or until it coats a metal spoon.

- Refrigerate at once, dividing large amounts into shallow containers so that it cools quickly.
- Precautions should also be taken with Hollandaise sauce, mousse, and any other recipes calling for raw or lightly cooked eggs. Use pasteurized egg products, or ensure that egg-mixtures reach a temperature of 160 degrees F.
- Note: Commercial, ready-made eggnog is prepared using pasteurized eggs and does not require heating. However, like homemade eggnog, it must be kept in the refrigerator.

## CHRISTMAS/NEW YEAR'S

Serving roast beef: The rule when cooking to "rare" appearance is to take internal temperature to 145 degrees F. **Poultry must be cooked to 180 degrees F.**

## TO SUM UP: SAFE HOLIDAY FOOD

- Thawing a Frozen Turkey: Don't thaw on the kitchen counter. Thaw in the microwave or refrigerator.
- Snacking: Snacking off the turkey is fine, but don't leave it out for more than 2 hours.
- Leftovers: To speed cooling, de-bone the turkey and refrigerate it in small, shallow containers.
- Cooking: Don't cook turkey overnight at low temperatures. Cook at 325 degrees F.
- Desserts: Cook custard to 160 degrees F and refrigerate pies made with eggs.
- Eggnog: Don't use a raw egg recipe. Use commercially prepared, pasteurized eggnog or make your own with cooked custard base.
- Cookies: Don't eat raw cookie dough if made with raw eggs.
- Cook fish until it flakes easily with a fork. A calibrated thermometer is one of the most important tools in a home kitchen just as it is in any commercial one. Look for tangible signs of doneness, such as aroma, appearance, radiation of heat.

# Transporting Food Out of Your Kitchen

The University of New Hampshire Cooperative Extension offers ways to keep potluck meals safe when taking them from your kitchen to another location.

Cases of foodborne illness start in home kitchens not because of the food but by how the food was prepared.

## WHY IS THERE A POTENTIAL PROBLEM WITH POTLUCK MEALS?

There is the potential for food handling errors at potluck meals. Some of the more obvious might include leaving perishable food at room temperature too long, cooking large amounts of food ahead of time and cooling it improperly, or failing to keep hot foods hot and cold foods cold. Other factors to consider are: how was the dish prepared prior to the event? What safe food handling practices were adhered to?

## WHAT SHOULD I TAKE TO THE POTLUCK TO REDUCE THE RISKS ASSOCIATED WITH FOODBORNE ILLNESS?

Here's what you should think about before you decide what to pack:

- Is there a place with clear running water where you and the other guests may wash their hands before and after serving and eating?

- Where can work surfaces and utensils be washed? Always use clean utensils to serve food.

**About Hot Foods**

- When you are cooking the food, cook it thoroughly. Cook red meats to 160 degrees F and poultry to 180 degrees F. Use a food thermometer to check doneness.
- Completely cook fish, meat, and poultry at one time—never partially cook any dish to warm later.
- Don't use recipes in which raw eggs remain raw or are only partially cooked.
- Serve casseroles as soon as you arrive or return at once to the oven.
- If the item is perishable, will you be able to keep it cold or hot until it is served? Perishable foods are those that require refrigeration: meat, poultry, fish, shellfish, egg or milk products and processed foods labeled "keep refrigerated."
- Will you be able to heat the food or keep it warmed to the proper temperature once you arrive at the event?
- When you cook food ahead of time, divide large portions of food into small, shallow containers for refrigeration. This ensures safe, rapid cooling.
- Use a warming unit to keep hot foods above 140 degrees F.
- To take a turkey to a pot luck: roast the bird unstuffed; carve the meat off the carcass, cover, and chill thoroughly. To reheat at the potluck, place the sliced turkey in an oven-safe baking dish, add about 1/2-cup water, cover with glass lid, and heat in a 350 degree F oven about 30 to 45 minutes or until well-heated through.

**About Cold Foods**

- Make sure that there will be refrigeration available at the event so that food can keep cold at the proper temperature. If you won't be able to keep cold foods cold and hot foods hot, consider taking food that needs no refrigeration, such as bread, cookies, chips, pretzels, or whole fruit.
- Transport cold foods in ice or cold packs to keep cold foods cold to 40 degrees F or below.
- Keep food in the refrigerator or on ice until served.
- Never leave perishable food out of the refrigerator for more than two hours.

**About Leftovers**

- Any leftover perishable foods should be thrown out.

# Plan a Food-Safe Easter Egg Hunt

**Before the Hunt**

- Consider buying one set of eggs for decorating only and another set for eating.
- Wash your hands thoroughly before handling eggs at every preparation step, including cooking, cooling, dyeing, and hiding.
- Only use eggs that have been refrigerated and discard eggs that are cracked or dirty.
- When cooking, place a single layer of eggs in a saucepan. Add water to at least one inch above the eggs. Cover the pan, bring the water to a boil, and carefully remove the pan from the heat. Let the eggs stand (18 minutes for extra-large eggs, 15 minutes for large, 12 minutes for medium). Immediately run cold water over the eggs. When the eggs are cool enough to handle, place them in an uncovered container in the refrigerator where they can air-dry.

  **Note: Air-cooled eggs are less hazardous than eggs cooled in water.**

- Keep hard-cooked Easter eggs refrigerated until just before the hunt. Keep them fully chilled by storing them on a shelf inside the refrigerator, not in the refrigerator door.
- When decorating, be sure to use food-grade dyes. It is safe to use commercial egg dyes, liquid food coloring, and fruit-drink powders. When handling eggs, be careful not to crack them. Otherwise, bacteria could enter the egg through the cracks in the shell.

**During the Hunt**

- Hide the eggs in places that are protected from dirt, pets, and other potential sources of bacteria.
- To prevent bacterial growth, don't let eggs sit in hiding places for more than two hours.

**After the Hunt**

- Discard any eggs that were cracked, dirty, or that children didn't find within two hours.
- Place the eggs back in the refrigerator until it's time to eat!

## Coloring Easter Eggs

Occasionally, eggs with clean, uncracked shells can be contaminated with bacteria. If foods containing harmful bacteria are consumed, they can cause foodborne illness. That's why it's important to cook eggs thoroughly and use a food thermometer to make sure egg-containing foods reach a safe internal temperature.

- Coloring Easter eggs can be fun for the whole family. Put two cups of water in each container and heat to almost boiling. Add two tablespoons of vinegar and 3 to 4 tablespoons of chopped herbs or vegetables. Allow to steep for 15 to 20 minutes to develop the color.
- While the liquid is still warm, dip hard-cooked eggs in the dye. When handling the eggs, wear rubber gloves or use a mesh strainer.

Like all perishable foods, such as meat, poultry, seafood, and produce, eggs need to be handled properly to prevent foodborne illness.

This Easter, revive the art of dyeing eggs in softer colors using natural dyes. Here are several herbs and vegetables you can use:

Light Yellow: carrot tops, orange, or lemon peel

Golden Yellow: turmeric, calendula, or marigold petals

Light Green: tansy, parsley, purple basil

Pink or Rose: rue, shredded beets, crushed cranberries

Lavender to Red: red onion skins

Blue: shredded purple cabbage, blueberries

Tan or Brown: tea leaves, coffee grounds

# Dashboard Dining

With more people eating in their vehicles, the car has become a popular site for snacking, or, what the American Dietetic Association (ADA) and ConAgra Foods call "dashboard dining." Here a few of their simple tips to ensure travel plans aren't ruined by a bad case of food poisoning.

"The key to safe 'dashboard dining' is bringing foods that are easy to carry, store, and eat," said Carolyn O'Neil, registered dietitian and home food-safety expert. "Take the time to think ahead and bring a supply of shelf-stable foods that are also nutritious. This way, car travelers can safely enjoy favorite foods in the car."

Ideas for quick, shelf-stable, and easy foods to take on the road include:

- Breads/grains: single-serving boxes of cereal, trail mix, energy bars, granola bars, cereal bars, bagels, muffins, crackers, popcorn, and chips.
- Fruits and vegetables: carrot and celery sticks and other cut-up raw vegetables, grapes, single-serve applesauce, whole fruit (apples, peaches, bananas), dried fruit mix, and juice boxes.
- Dairy and alternatives: single-serve milk or soy beverage boxes and pudding cups.
- Meat and other protein sources: cans of tuna, peanut butter (for sandwiches or with celery and apples), nuts, and single-serve packages of peanut butter and crackers or cheese and crackers.
- Water: bottles of water

## TRAVELING WITH FOOD

- When traveling with food, keep hot foods hot and cold foods cold. Wrap hot food in foil and heavy towels, or insulated containers to maintain a temperature of at least 140 degrees F. Store cold foods in a cooler with ice or freezer packs so they remain at 40 degrees F or lower. Full coolers keep their temperature longer than only partially filled ones.
- When traveling or picnicking away from home, it's important to take along the basic food safety necessities and follow these helpful tips:
  - If water for hand washing is not available, take along disposable wipes.
  - Like all perishables, eggs need to be kept cold. When hosting an outdoor celebration, store cold egg dishes in the cooler, along with a cold pack or ice.
  - When traveling, transport the cooler in the air-conditioned passenger compartment of your car, rather than in a hot trunk. Don't let egg dishes sit out for more than two hours. On a hot day (90 degrees F higher), reduce this time to one hour.

## TIPS FOR PERISHABLE FOODS

- If transporting perishable foods [i.e., cheese sticks, yogurt, and yogurt drinks], pack them in plenty of ice in a well-insulated cooler or with cooling packs in a well-insulated lunch bag.
- As an extra safety precaution, keep a refrigerator thermometer inside the cooler at all times. Make sure the cooler is set below 40 degrees F. to ensure safe food storage.

Note: In regions with cold weather, transport the cooler in the trunk, which is the coolest part of the car in the wintertime.

In warmer weather, transport the cooler in an air-conditioned car instead of in a hot trunk. Also:

- When preparing perishable items to transport, do not partially cook foods.
- Partial cooking of foods ahead of time allows bacteria to survive and multiply to the point that subsequent cooking may not destroy harmful bacteria.
- Cook meat/poultry completely and place in a cooler that is below 40 degrees F. Make sure to reheat foods to an internal temperature of 165 degrees F.

Remember to watch the clock when eating food in a hot car. Perishable foods should not stay out of the refrigerator for more than two hours. When the temperature is 90 degrees F. or warmer, that time is reduced to *one* hour.

## HOW TO KEEP HANDS AND EATING SURFACES
## CLEAN OUTDOORS

- Always wash hands thoroughly, especially after activities such as filling your vehicle with gas, stopping at a rest area, or changing a child's diaper.
- Stop at a restaurant, gas station, or rest area to wash hands, using warm, soapy water (washing for at least 20 seconds), or bring a pack of moist towelettes or spray bottle of soap and water solution with paper towels in the car.
- Be sure everyone washes hands before handling or eating foods in the car.
- Keep a stash of eating utensils in the car (i.e., plastic utensils, straws, napkins, garbage bags, and paper towels).

# Great Advice for an Enjoyable and Safe Picnic

Contributors: Scottie Misner, PhD, RD and Ralph Meer, PhD, RD, The University of Arizona Cooperative Extension

Keeping food safe to eat outdoors is as simple as keeping hot foods hot, cold foods cold, and all foods clean. Several options exist for keeping coolers cold.

Ice: Commercial ice is available in cubes or blocks. A block will last longer than an equal weight of ice cubes. Ice can be made at home. Fill clean half-gallon milk cartons, juice cartons or jugs 2/3 full of drinking water. Put lids on and freeze. This water, when thawed, can be used to make coffee and tea.

Sealed refrigerant (blue ice): These purchased blocks freeze several degrees colder than ice and can be used in place of ice. In addition, they can be refrozen and reused.

Frozen food: Freezing meat and juices before packing them in a cooler will also help keep other foods cold. Frozen food will thaw gradually and be ready for grilling or cooking. Wrap meat thoroughly so juices won't drip on other foods.

Keep foods cold: Foodborne illness bacteria grow very rapidly on these foods. Do not let them make you and your family sick.

Perishable foods: Pack these foods closest to the ice in a cooler. Pack the foods you will eat first on top so you can work your way down during the meal. Store the cooler in a shady area and avoid unnecessary opening of the cooler.

Leftovers: After grilling, store leftovers as soon as possible in your cooler. Do not let food cool first. Keep foods clean: Since bacteria live all around us, and even on our bodies, always wash and dry your hands before handling food or cooking.

Taking the temperature of a hamburger on my grill is much easier than the thought of blaming myself for undercooking my child's last meal. Some of you may think that's overdoing it, but I would rather ensure that I will not experience the same pain and burden as those parents who did not know the risks at the time and lost their beloved children.

**Tom Dominick, one of our Baker's Dozen.**

# Tips on Packing a Safe and Nutritious School Lunch

As you send your children off to school with bag lunches or lunchboxes in hand, you need to consider what will be safe to eat after being out of the refrigerator for many hours.

Here are some suggestions for some essential tips for safe and nutritious "packed" school lunches:

**Preparation**

- Wash your hands and all surfaces and utensils before preparing a lunch. Hot soapy water can get rid of bacteria. If your child uses a lunch box, make sure it is cleaned before each use.
- Do not include food that looks bad or has even the smallest spot of mold. When in doubt, throw it out.
- Be sure to wash fruits and vegetables in cool running water before packing.
- Keep family pets away from food preparation areas.

---

The Alliance for Food and Farming, an educational clearinghouse on food safety funded by a coalition of farmers and produce organizations, has released information for parents of schoolchildren on packing a safe and nutritious lunch for school. The tips include advice on safe handling and preparation of bag/lunchbox lunches, and nutritious ideas for including fruits, vegetables, and nuts in lunches. Also the list provided some top websites for different fruit and vegetable websites with fun projects and/or recipes for children.

- Perishable food should have been well-refrigerated at home before including in the lunch box, and will need to be stored with a freezer gel pack in an insulated lunch bag if used. Many fruits and vegetables are terrific choices as they don't require refrigeration, but cut-up fruit will need to be kept cold.
- Avoid cross-contamination—this is one of the largest single causes of foodborne contamination in the home. When preparing sandwiches, be sure to wash the board after using it to cut raw meat or poultry, and before using it for food that will not be cooked such as lettuce, tomatoes, and bread.
- Perishable food such as salads or cut fruit should not be left out at room temperature for more than 2 hours (and less than 1 hour if the temperature is above 90 degrees F). It's fine to prepare food the night before and pack lunch in the refrigerator. Freezing sandwiches can help them stay cold. However, for the best quality, don't freeze sandwiches containing lettuce, tomatoes, or mayonnaise.
- Teach children to wash their hands before eating, even away from home.
- If the child suspects anything smells bad or tastes odd or cold foods or perishable foods have become warm, instruct the child to show care and throw out anything that is suspect.
- Toss food packaging or paper bags. Do not reuse packaging because it could contaminate other food and cause foodborne illness.
- For children with allergies, instruct them to be cautious when "sharing" lunches with other children to avoid items that can make them ill.

# PART FOUR

# Coping with Crises

# What To Do If You or a Family Member Develops a Foodborne Illness

What if you or a member of your family develops a foodborne illness? According to the Mayo Clinic, Scottsdale, Arizona: "Rest and drink plenty of liquids. Don't use antidiarrhea medications because they may slow elimination of the bacteria from your system. Mild to moderate illness often resolves on its own. However, if you have severe symptoms such as excessive nausea and vomiting, bloody diarrhea or a high temperature, or belong to a high-risk group, seek help in nearest emergency room or call your doctor at once."

Preserve the evidence. Securely wrap a portion of the suspected food, mark it "Danger," and then refrigerate it. Save all the packaging material, cans, cartons, as well as any identical unopened products.

Make a list of the foods you have eaten for the last three days. Write down the type of food, the date and time consumed, and when the symptoms began. Usually the last thing you ate, as most people believe, did not cause the illness. Also, people usually only think about meals from a restaurant as the source of illness. But as you learned from the Nancy Donley story at the beginning of this book, people frequently become ill from foods cooked at home. Some foodborne illnesses, such as Hepatitis A, may take up to six weeks to develop.

Call your health department if the suspect food was served at a large gathering such as a church picnic, or in a restaurant or any other food establishment or if it is a commercial product. Call the USDA Meat and Poultry Hotline, 1-800-535-4555, if the suspect food is a USDA-inspected product and you have all of the packaging.

Our informative forensic sanitarian, Dr. Powitz, reminds us that if a meat product has been cut and trimmed, the USDA inspection stamp will be absent. Therefore, there is no way to know where the product came from.

# *What To Do When the Refrigerator Goes Off*

Sooner or later, every home has a power outage. The electricity may have gone off during a snowstorm or thunderstorm, or the refrigerator may simply quit working. Whatever the cause, dealing with the food involved when the unit is off requires a knowledge of food safety.

**Prepare in Advance for All Power Outages**
- If you live in an area where loss of electricity from summer or winter storms is a problem, you can plan ahead to be prepared for the worst. Stock up on shelf-stable foods: canned goods, juices, and "no-freeze" entrees.
- Plan ahead how you can keep foods cold. Buy some freeze-pak inserts and keep them frozen. Buy a cooler. Freeze water in plastic containers or store bags of ice. Know in advance where you can buy dry and block ice. Develop emergency freezer-sharing plans with friends in another part of town or in a nearby area.
- The key to determining the safety of foods in the refrigerator and freezer is knowing how cold they are. The refrigerator temperature should be 40 degrees F or below; the freezer, 0 degrees F or lower.

**During a Power Outage**
- Do not open the refrigerator door for two hours in case the power comes on.
- Keep the freezer door closed. "Best advice," says Dr. Powitz, our forensic sanitarian, "is leave the freezer alone. The more you open and close the

door, the more problems you will have." Keep what cold air you have inside. Don't open the door any more than necessary. You'll be relieved to know that a full freezer will stay at freezing temperatures about 2 days; a half-full freezer about 1 day.

- If your freezer is not full, group packages so they form an "igloo" to protect each other. Place them to one side or on a tray so that if they begin thawing, their juices won't get on other food. And, if you think power will be out for several days, find some dry ice and put it in the refrigerator and its freezer.

## Handling Dry Ice

- Know in advance where you can buy dry ice. Some grocery stores carry dry ice. Check there. To locate a distributor of dry ice, look under "ice" or "carbon dioxide" in the phone book. A 25-pound block of dry ice will keep a 10-cubic-foot freezer full of food safe 3 to 4 days; half-full, 2 to 3 days.
- A full 18-cubic-foot freezer requires 50 to 100 pounds of dry ice to keep food safe 2 days; half-full, less than 2 days. Handle dry ice with caution and in a well-ventilated area. Don't touch it with bare hands; wear gloves or use tongs.
- Wrap dry ice in brown paper for longer storage. One large piece lasts longer than small ones.
- The temperature of dry ice is **minus** 216 degrees F; therefore, it may cause freezer burn on items located near or touching it. Separate dry ice from the food using a piece of cardboard.

If the electricity is off for more than two hours, proceed to throw away the following foods if kept for more than two hours above 40 degrees F:

- Both raw and cooked meats, poultry, fish, eggs, and egg substitutes as well as milk, cream, yogurt, or soft cheese, such as brie or camembert, deli meat, hot dogs, creamy salad dressings, custard, chiffon or cheese pies, refrigerator cookie dough, opened jars of mayonnaise, tartar sauce, or horseradish. Look at the fruits and vegetables for signs of rot.
- Save the following foods, unless they have turned moldy or have an unusual odor: butter or margarine, hard or processed cheese, fresh fruit and vegetables (unpeeled, uncut), opened jars of vinegar-based dressings, jelly, relish, salsa, barbecue sauce, mustard, catsup, olives, peanut butter, fruit pies, bread, rolls, or muffins.
- Refreeze thawed food that still contains ice crystals or feels cold. Unless you put your cold items in a cooler with a cold source such as ice, they could have been in the temperature danger zone too long.
- The advice given is conservative because it takes away the element of guessing on the part of the homeowner. "When in doubt, throw it out"

takes the burden and decision making off the shoulders of those victims in a disaster situation.

- Never taste food to determine its safety! Some foods may look and smell fine, but if they've been at room temperature for more than two hours, bacteria that cause foodborne illness can begin to grow very rapidly. Some types of bacteria produce toxins that are not destroyed when the food is reheated.

- Even if food has started to thaw, some foods can be kept safely: The foods in your freezer that partially or completely thaw before the power is restored may be safely refrozen if they still contain ice crystals or are 40 degrees F. or below. You will have to evaluate each item separately. Generally, be very careful with meat and poultry products or any food containing milk, cream, sour cream, or soft cheese. Again, "When in doubt, throw it out."

Keep the door closed as much as possible. Discard any perishable foods (such as meat, poultry, fish, eggs, and leftovers) that have been above 40 degrees F. for two hours or more.

Keep an appliance thermometer in both the refrigerator and freezer. This will remove the guesswork of just how cold the unit is because it will give you the exact temperature.

These are rule-of-thumb guides.

Be sure to discard any fully cooked items in either the freezer or the refrigerator that have come into contact with raw meat juices. Remember, you can't rely on appearance or odor.

Never taste food to determine its safety! Some foods may look and smell fine, but if they've been at room temperature too long, bacteria that cause foodborne illness can begin to grow very rapidly. Some types will produce toxins that are not destroyed by cooking.

# *Other Kitchen Contaminants*

## Lead Poisoning

Lead leached from some types of ceramic dinnerware into foods and beverages is often consumers' biggest source of dietary lead. Here are some tips to reduce your exposure:

- Don't store acidic foods, such as fruit juices, in ceramic containers.
- Avoid or limit to special occasions the use of antique or collectible housewares for food and beverages. Never use cracked or checked ceramic dinnerware or drinking containers.
- Follow label directions on ornamental ceramic products labeled "Not for Food Use—May Poison Food" or "For Decorative Purposes Only," and don't use these items for preparing or storing food. Also, don't store beverages in lead crystal containers for extended periods.
- High temperature use of some microwave food packaging material may cause packaging components, such as paper, adhesives, and polymers, to migrate into food at excessive levels. For that reason, choose only microwave-safe cooking containers. Never use packaging cartons for cooking unless the package directs you to do so.

### Insect and Rodent Droppings, and Dirt
- Wash the tops of cans with soap and water before opening and dry thoroughly.

- Avoid storing food in cabinets that are under the sink or have water, drain, and heating pipes passing through them. Food stored here can attract insects and rodents through openings that are difficult to seal adequately.
- Contact a local pest control if the problem continues.

**Controlling Rodents and Flies**

- Keep doors and windows closed, or be sure the screens are in good repair.
- Clean trash cans daily. Be sure their covers fit tightly.
- Keep trash and garbage off the floors.
- Keep storage areas clean.
- Never leave food out at night. Mop the floors and take out the trash before retiring.

# PART FIVE

# When You Want To Know More

# Contact the Cooperative Extension Office in Your State

Cooperative Extension is a nationwide informal education system. It provides practical, research-based information and education for families, youth, communities, and agriculture. Educational programs include 4-H youth development, nutrition and food safety, environmental and water quality, family life skills, agriculture production, leadership development, home gardening, and many others. Cooperative Extension, a national network, is based at each state's land grant universities, partnering with U.S. Department of Agriculture, local counties, volunteers, and organizations.

Check the government pages in your local phone book under the County or University for your local Cooperative Extension office or use this handy chart below for all 50 states and the District of Columbia:

**STATE EXTENSION SERVICE DIRECTORS/ADMINISTRATORS**

| STATE | ADDRESS | TELEPHONE AND FAX NUMBER |
| --- | --- | --- |
| AL | Alabama A&M University<br>P.O. Box 967<br>Normal, AL 35762 | 256/851-5943<br>(FAX) 256/851-5840 |
| AK | University of Alaska Fairbanks<br>P. O. Box 756180<br>Fairbanks, AK 99775-6180 | 907/474-7246<br>(FAX) 907/474-6971 |
| AZ | College of Agriculture<br>University of Arizona<br>Forbes Bldg., Rm. 301<br>Tucson, AZ 85721 | 520/621-7209<br>FAX: 520-621-1314 |

**STATE EXTENSION SERVICE DIRECTORS/ADMINISTRATORS (*cont.*)**

| STATE | ADDRESS | TELEPHONE AND FAX NUMBER |
|---|---|---|
| AR | University of Arkansas<br>Box 4990<br>1200 N. University Drive<br>Pine Bluff, AR 71611 | 870/543-8529/8534<br>(FAX) 870/543-8033 |
| CA | University of California<br>300 Lakeside Dr., 6th Fl.<br>Oakland, CA 94612-3560 | 510/987-0060<br>(FAX) 510/451-2317 |
| CO | Colorado State University<br>1 Administration Building<br>Fort Collins, CO 80523-4040 | 970/491-6281<br>(FAX) 970/491-6208 |
| CT | College of Agriculture & Natural Resources<br>University of Connecticut<br>Young Building, Rm 216<br>1376 Storrs Road, U-36<br>Storrs, CT 06269-4036 | 860/486-6271<br>(FAX) 860/486-4128 |
| DE | University of Delaware<br>127 Townsend Hall<br>Newark, DE 19717 | 302/831-2501<br>(FAX) 302/831-6758 |
| DC | University of the District of Columbia<br>4200 Connecticut Avenue, NW<br>Washington, D.C. 20008 | 202/274-7100<br>(FAX) 202/274-7016 |
| FL | Florida A&M University<br>Perry-Paige Building, Room 215<br>Tallahassee, FL 32307 | 850/599-3546<br>(FAX) 850/561-2151 |
| GA | Ft. Valley State University<br>P.O. Box 4061<br>1005 State University Drive<br>Ft. Valley, GA 31030-3298 | 912/825-6296<br>(FAX) 912/825-6299 |
| HI | University of Hawaii at Manoa/College of<br>Tropical Agriculture & Human Resources<br>3050 Maile Way, Room 202<br>Honolulu, HI 96822 | 808/956-8234<br>(FAX) 808/956-9105 |
| ID | University of Idaho<br>Twin Falls R&E Center<br>P.O. Box 1827<br>315 Falls Avenue<br>Twin Falls, ID 83303-1827 | 208/736-3603<br>(FAX) 208/736-0843 |
| IL | University of Illinois<br>123 Mumford Hall<br>1301 West Gregory Drive<br>Urbana, IL 61801 | 217/333-5900<br>(FAX) 217/244-5403 |
| IN | Purdue University<br>1140 Agriculture Admin. Bldg.<br>West Lafayette, IN 47907-1140 | 765/494-8489<br>(FAX) 765/494-5876 |
| IA | Iowa State University<br>101 Mac Kay<br>Ames, IA 50011-1120 | 800/262-3804 Answer Line<br>(FAX) 515/294-1040 |

**STATE EXTENSION SERVICE DIRECTORS/ADMINISTRATORS (*cont.*)**

| STATE | ADDRESS | TELEPHONE AND FAX NUMBER |
|---|---|---|
| KS | Kansas State University<br>123 Umberger Hall<br>Manhattan, KS 66506-3401 | 785/532-7137<br>(FAX) 785/532-6563 |
| KY | Kentucky State University<br>Coop. Ext. Program Facility<br>400 E. Main Street<br>Frankfort, KY 40601 | 502/227-6310<br>(FAX) 502/227-5933 |
| LA | Louisiana State University<br>P.O. Box 25100<br>Baton Rouge, LA 70894-5100 | 225/578-6083<br>225/578-4225 |
| ME | University of Maine<br>Cooperative Extension<br>5741 Libby Hall, Rm. 102<br>Orono, ME 04469-5741 | 207/581-2811<br>(FAX) 207/581-1387 |
| MD | University of Maryland<br>Eastern Shore<br>Princess Anne, MD 21853 | 410/651-6206<br>(FAX) 410/651-6207 |
| MA | Universiy of Massachusetts<br>212 Stockbridge Hall<br>Amherst, MA 01003 | 413/545-4800<br>(FAX) 413/545-6555 |
| MI | Michigan State University<br>108 Agriculture Hall<br>East Lansing, MI 48824-1039 | 517/355-2308<br>(FAX) 517/355-6473 |
| MN | University of Minnesota<br>Room 240 Coffey Hall<br>1420 Eckles Avenue<br>St. Paul, MN 55108-6070 | 612/624-2703<br>(FAX) 612/625-6227 |
| MS | Mississippi State University<br>Box 9601<br>Mississippi State, MS 39762-9601 | 662/325-3036<br>(FAX) 662/325-8407 |
| MO | University of Missouri<br>309 University Hall<br>Columbia, MO 65211-3020 | 573/882-7754<br>(FAX) 573/884-4204 |
| MT | Montana State University<br>204A Culbertson Hall<br>Bozeman, MT 59717-2230 | 406/994-6647<br>(FAX) 406/994-1756 |
| NE | University of Nebraska<br>211 Agriculture Hall<br>Lincoln, NE 68583-0703 | 402/472-2966<br>(FAX) 402/472-5557 |
| NV | University of Nevada<br>Cooperative Extension<br>Mail Stop 404<br>Reno, NV 89557 | 775/784-7070<br>(FAX) 775/784-4881 |
| NH | University of New Hampshire<br>59 College Road<br>103A Taylor Hall<br>Durham, NH 03824-3587 | 603/862-1520<br>(FAX) 603/862-1585 |

**STATE EXTENSION SERVICE DIRECTORS/ADMINISTRATORS (*cont.*)**

| STATE | ADDRESS | TELEPHONE AND FAX NUMBER |
|---|---|---|
| NJ | Rutgers University<br>88 Lippman Drive<br>New Brunswick, NJ 08901-8525 | 732/932-9306<br>(FAX) 732/932-6633 |
| NM | New Mexico State University<br>P.O. Box 30003<br>Department 3AE<br>Las Cruces, NM 88003 | 505/646-3016<br>(FAX) 505/646-5975 |
| NY | Cornell University<br>365 Roberts Hall<br>Ithaca, NY 14853-5905 | 607/255-2237<br>(FAX) 607/255-0788 |
| NC | North Carolina State University<br>Box 7602<br>Raleigh, NC 27695-7602 | 919/515-2811<br>(FAX) 919/515-3135 |
| ND | North Dakota State University<br>315 Morrill Hall, P.O. Box 5437<br>Fargo, ND 58105-5437 | 701/231-8944<br>(FAX) 701/231-8378 |
| OH | Ohio State University<br>3 Agricultural Admin. Bldg.<br>2120 Fyffe Road<br>Columbus, OH 43210 | 614/292-4067<br>(FAX) 614/688-3807 |
| OK | Oklahoma State University<br>139 Agriculture Hall<br>Stillwater, OK 74078-6019 | 405/744-5398<br>(FAX) 405/744-5339 |
| OR | Oregon State University<br>Extension Administration<br>101 Ballard Extension Hall<br>Corvallis, OR 97331-3606 | 541/737-2713<br>(FAX) 541/737-4423 |
| PA | The Pennsylvania State University<br>217 Ag. Admin. Bldg.<br>University Park, PA 16802 | 814/863-3438<br>(FAX) 814/863-7905 |
| RI | University of Rhode Island<br>College of the Environment and Life Sciences<br>12 Woodward Hall<br>9 East Alumni Avenue<br>Kingston, RI 02881 | 401/874-2954<br>(FAX) 401/874-4017 |
| SC | Clemson University<br>103 Barre Hall<br>Clemson, SC 29634-0310 | 864/656-3382<br>(FAX) 864/656-0765 |
| SD | South Dakota State University<br>P.O. Box 2207D, Ag. Hall 154<br>Brookings, SD 57007 | 605/688-4792<br>(FAX) 605/688-6347 |
| TN | Tennessee State University<br>3500 John A. Merritt Building<br>Nashville, TN 37209-1561 | 615/963-5526<br>(FAX) 615/963-5394 |
| TX | Texas A&M University<br>Jack K. Williams Administration Bldg.<br>Room 113<br>College Station, TX 77843-2147 | 409/845-4747<br>(FAX) 409/862-1637 |

**STATE EXTENSION SERVICE DIRECTORS/ADMINISTRATORS (*cont.*)**

| STATE | ADDRESS | TELEPHONE AND FAX NUMBER |
|---|---|---|
| UT | Utah State University<br>4900 Old Main Hill<br>Logan, UT 84322-4900 | 435/797-2201<br>(FAX)435/797-3268 |
| VT | University of Vermont Extension Systems<br>601 Main Street<br>Burlington, VT 05401-3439 | 802/656-2980<br>(FAX) 802/656-8642 |
| VA | Virginia Polytechnic Institute and State University<br>Office of the Director<br>101 Hutcheson Hall<br>Blacksburg, VA 24061-0402 | 540/231-5299<br>(FAX) 540/231-4370 |
| WA | Washington State University<br>P.O. Box 646230<br>411 Hulbert Hall<br>Pullman, WA 99164-6230 | 509/335-2933<br>(FAX) 509/335-2926 |
| WV | West Virginia University<br>P.O. Box 6031<br>Morgantown, WV 26506-6031 | 304/293-5691<br>(FAX) 304/293-7163 |
| WI | University of Wisconsin<br>432 N. Lake Street<br>Room 601, Extension Building<br>Madison, WI 53706-1498 | 608/263-2775<br>(FAX) 608/265-4545 |
| WY | University of Wyoming<br>College of Agriculture<br>Room 103, P.O. Box 3354<br>Laramie, WY 82071-3354 | 307/766-5124<br>(FAX) 307/766-3998 |

# If You Want
# To Learn More
# About Food Safety

So many people who read this book in advance of publication have suggested that more information about foodborne diseases be discussed. The following facts were obtained from the Centers for Disease Control and Prevention.

## WHAT CAUSES FOODBORNE ILLNESS?

Foodborne illness is caused by consuming contaminated foods or beverages. These different diseases have many different symptoms, so there is no one "syndrome." However, the microbe or toxin enters the body through the gastrointestinal tract, and often causes the first symptoms there, so nausea, vomiting, abdominal cramps, and diarrhea are common symptoms in many foodborne diseases.

## WHAT ARE THE MOST COMMON
## FOODBORNE DISEASES?

The most commonly recognized foodborne infections are those caused by the bacteria *campylobacter, salmonella, E. coli O157:H7*, and by a group of viruses called *calicivirus,* also known as the Norwalk and Norwalk-like viruses.

- *Campylobacter* is a bacterial pathogen that causes fever, diarrhea, and abdominal cramps. It is the most commonly identified bacterial cause of diarrheal illness in the world. These bacteria live in the intestines of healthy birds, and most raw poultry meat has *campylobacter* on it. Eating under-cooked chicken, or other food that has been contaminated with juices dripping from raw chicken, is the most frequent source of this infection.

- *Salmonella* is also a bacterium that is widespread in the intestines of birds, reptiles, and mammals. It can spread to humans via a variety of different foods of animal origin. The illness it causes, *salmonellosis,* typically includes fever, diarrhea, and abdominal cramps. In persons with poor underlying health or weakened immune systems, it can invade the bloodstream and cause life-threatening infections.

- *E. coli O157:H7* is a bacterial pathogen that has a reservoir in cattle and other similar animals. Human illness typically follows consumption of food or water that has been contaminated with microscopic amounts of cow feces. The illness it causes is often a severe and bloody diarrhea and painful abdominal cramps, without much fever. In 3% to 5% of cases, a serious complication called hemolytic uremic syndrome (HUS) can occur several weeks after the initial symptoms, and includes temporary anemia, profuse bleeding, and kidney failure.

- *Calicivirus,* or Norwalk-like virus is an extremely common cause of foodborne illness, though it is rarely diagnosed, because the laboratory test is not widely available. It causes an acute gastrointestinal illness, usually with more vomiting than diarrhea that resolves within two days.

- Unlike many foodborne pathogens that have animal reservoirs, it is believed that Norwalk-like viruses spread primarily from one infected person to another. Infected cooks can contaminate a salad or sandwich as they prepare it, if they have the virus on their hands. Infected fishermen have contaminated oysters as they harvested them.

In addition to disease caused by direct infection, some foodborne diseases are caused by the presence of a toxin in the food that was produced by a microbe in the food.

- For example, the bacterium *Staphylococcus aureus* can grow in some foods and produce a toxin that causes intense vomiting. The rare but deadly disease botulism occurs when the bacterium *Clostridium botulinum* grows and produces a powerful paralytic toxin in foods. These toxins can produce illness even if the microbes that produced them are no longer there.

- Other toxins and poisonous chemicals can cause foodborne illness. People can become ill if a pesticide is inadvertently added to a food, or if naturally poisonous substances are used to prepare a meal.

- Every year, people become ill after mistaking poisonous mushrooms for safe species, or after eating poisonous reef fishes.

The spectrum of foodborne diseases is constantly changing. A century ago, typhoid fever, tuberculosis, and cholera were common foodborne diseases.

Improvements in food safety, such as pasteurization of milk, safe canning, and the disinfection of water supplies have conquered those diseases.

Today other foodborne infections have taken their place, including some that have only recently been discovered.

- In the last 15 years, several important diseases of unknown cause have turned out to be complications of foodborne infections. For example, we now know that the Guillain-Barre syndrome can be caused by *campylobacter* infection, and that the most common cause of acute kidney failure in children, hemolytic uremic syndrome, is caused by infection with *E. coli O157:H7* and related bacteria. In the future, other diseases whose origins are currently unknown may turn out be related to foodborne infections.

## WHEN TO CONSULT YOUR DOCTOR ABOUT A DIARRHEAL ILLNESS

A health-care provider should be consulted for a diarrheal illness that lasts for more 3 days and is accompanied by high fever (temperature over 101.5 degrees F, measured orally), blood in the stools, prolonged vomiting that prevents keeping liquids down which can lead to dehydration, signs of dehydration, including a decrease in urination, dry mouth and throat, and feeling dizzy when standing up.

## HOW MANY CASES OF FOODBORNE DISEASE ARE THERE IN THE UNITED STATES?

An estimated 76 million cases of foodborne disease occur each year in the United States. The great majority of these cases is mild and cause symptoms for only a day or two. Some cases are more serious, and CDC estimates that there are 325,000 hospitalizations and 5,200 deaths related to foodborne diseases each year. The most severe cases tend to occur in the very old, the very young, those who have an illness already that reduces their immune system function, and in healthy people exposed to a very high dose of organism.

## HOW DO PUBLIC HEALTH DEPARTMENTS TRACK FOODBORNE DISEASES?

Routine monitoring of important diseases by public health departments is called disease surveillance. Each state decides which diseases are to be under surveillance in that state.

In most states, diagnosed cases of *salmonellosis, E. coli O157:H7,* and other serious infections are routinely reported to the health department. The county reports them to the state health department that reports them to CDC.

Tens of thousands of cases of these "notifiable conditions" are reported every year. For example, nearly 35,000 cases of *salmonella* infection were reported to CDC in 1998.

However, most foodborne infections go undiagnosed and unreported, either because the ill person does not see a doctor, or the doctor does not make a specific diagnosis. Also, infections with some microbes are not reportable in the first place.

To get more information about infections that might be diagnosed but not reported, CDC developed a special surveillance system called FoodNet. FoodNet provides the best available information about specific foodborne infections in the United States, and summarizes them in an annual report. In addition to tracking the number of reported cases of individual infections, states also collect information about foodborne outbreaks, and report a summary of that information to CDC.

About 400 to 500 foodborne outbreaks investigated by local and state health departments are reported each year. This includes information about many diseases that are not notifiable and thus are not under individual surveillance, so it provides some useful general information about foodborne illnesses.

## WHAT ARE FOODBORNE DISEASE OUTBREAKS AND WHY DO THEY OCCUR?

An outbreak of foodborne illness occurs when a group of people consume the same contaminated food and two or more of them come down with the same illness. It may be a group that ate a meal together somewhere, or it may be a group of people who do not know each other at all, but who all happened to buy and eat the same contaminated item from a grocery store or restaurant.

For an outbreak to occur, something must have happened to contaminate a batch of food that was eaten by a group of people. Often, a combination of events contributes to the outbreak. A contaminated food may be left out at room temperature for many hours, allowing the bacteria to multiply to high numbers, and then be insufficiently cooked to kill the bacteria.

Many outbreaks are local in nature. They are recognized when a group of people realize that they all became ill after a common meal, and someone calls the local health department. This classic local outbreak might follow a catered meal at a reception, a pot-luck supper, or eating a meal at an understaffed restaurant on a particularly busy day. However, outbreaks are increasingly being recognized that are more widespread, that affect persons in many different places, and that are spread out over several weeks.

The vast majority of reported cases of foodborne illness is not part of recognized outbreaks, but occurs as individual or "sporadic" cases. It may be that many of these cases are actually part of unrecognized widespread or diffuse outbreaks. Detecting and investigating such widespread outbreaks is a major challenge to our public health system. This is the reason that new and more sophisticated laboratory methods are being used at CDC and in state public health department laboratories.

## HOW DOES FOOD BECOME CONTAMINATED?

We live in a microbial world, and there are many opportunities for food to become contaminated as it is produced and prepared. Many foodborne microbes are present in healthy animals (usually in their intestines) raised for food. Meat and poultry carcasses can become contaminated during slaughter by contact with small amounts of intestinal contents. Similarly, fresh fruits and vegetables can be contaminated if they are washed or irrigated with water that is contaminated with animal manure or human sewage.

- Some types of *salmonella* can infect a hen's ovary so that the internal contents of a normal looking egg can be contaminated with salmonella even before the shell in formed.
- Oysters and other filter-feeding shellfish can concentrate *vibrio* bacteria that are naturally present in sea water, or other microbes that are present in human sewage dumped into the sea.

Later in food processing, other foodborne microbes can be introduced from infected humans who handle the food or by cross-contamination from some other raw agricultural product.

- For example, *Shigella* bacteria, *hepatitis A virus,* and *Norwalk virus* can be introduced by the unwashed hands of people handling food who are themselves infected.
- In the kitchen, microbes can be transferred from one food to another food by using the same knife, cutting board, or other utensil to prepare both without washing the surface or utensil in between.
- A food that is fully cooked can become recontaminated if it touches other raw foods or drippings from raw foods that contain pathogens.
- The way that food is handled after it is contaminated can also make a difference in whether or not an outbreak occurs. Many bacterial microbes need to multiply to a larger number before enough are present in food to cause disease. Given warm moist conditions and an ample supply of nutrients, one bacterium that reproduces by dividing itself every half-hour can produce 16 billion progeny in 12 hours.

As a result, lightly contaminated food left out overnight can be highly infectious by the next day. If the food were refrigerated promptly, the bacteria would not multiply at all. However, in general, refrigeration or freezing prevents virtually all bacteria from growing but generally preserves them in a state of suspended animation. This general rule has a few surprising exceptions.

- Two foodborne bacteria, *Listeria monocytogenes* and *Yersinia enterocolitica* can actually grow at refrigerator temperatures. High-salt, high-sugar, or high-acid levels keep bacteria from growing, which is why salted meats, jam, and pickled vegetables are traditional preserved foods.

Microbes are killed by heat. If food is heated to an internal temperature above 160 degrees F. for even a few seconds, this is sufficient to kill parasites, viruses or bacteria.

- The exception is the *clostridium* bacteria, which produce a heat-resistant form called a spore. *Clostridium* spores are killed only at temperatures above boiling. This is why canned foods must be cooked to a high temperature under pressure as part of the canning process. The toxins produced by bacteria vary in their sensitivity to heat.
- The *staphylococcal* toxin, which causes vomiting, is not killed even if it is boiled.
- Fortunately, the potent toxin that causes botulism is completely inactivated by boiling.

## WHAT FOODS ARE MOST ASSOCIATED WITH FOODBORNE ILLNESS?

Raw foods of animal origin are the most likely to be contaminated; that is, raw meat and poultry, raw eggs, unpasteurized milk, and raw shellfish. Because filter-feeding shellfish strain microbes from the sea over many months, they are particularly likely to be contaminated if there are any pathogens in the seawater. Foods that mingle the products of many individual animals, such as bulk raw milk, pooled raw eggs, or ground beef, are particularly hazardous because a pathogen present in any one of the animals may contaminate the whole batch. A single hamburger may contain meat from hundreds of animals.

A single restaurant omelet may contain eggs from hundreds of chickens. A glass of raw milk may contain milk from hundreds of cows. A broiler chicken carcass can be exposed to the drippings and juices of many thousands of other birds that went through the same cold water tank after slaughter.

## Fruits and Vegetables

When consumed raw, fruits and vegetables are a particular concern. Washing can decrease but not eliminate contamination, so the home cooks can do little to protect themselves.

Recently, a number of outbreaks have been traced to fresh fruits and vegetables that were processed under less than sanitary conditions. These outbreaks show that the quality of the water used for washing and chilling the produce after it is harvested is critical. Using water that is not clean can contaminate many boxes of produce.

- Fresh manure used to fertilize vegetables can also contaminate them. Alfalfa sprouts and other raw sprouts pose a particular challenge, as the conditions under which they are sprouted are ideal for growing microbes as well as sprouts, and because they are eaten without further cooking. That means that a few bacteria present on the seeds can grow to high numbers of pathogens on the sprouts.
- Unpasteurized fruit juice can also be contaminated if there are pathogens in or on the fruit that is used to make it.

## WHAT CAN HOME COOKS DO TO PROTECT THEIR FAMILIES AND THEMSELVES FROM FOODBORNE ILLNESS?

A few simple precautions can reduce the risk of foodborne diseases:

*Cook:* Meat, poultry, and eggs thoroughly. Using a thermometer to measure the internal temperature of meat is a good way to be sure that it is cooked sufficiently to kill bacteria. For example, ground beef should be cooked to an internal temperature of 160 degrees F. Eggs should be cooked until the yolk is firm.

*Separate:* Don't cross-contaminate one food with another. Avoid cross-contaminating foods by washing hands, utensils, and cutting boards after they have been in contact with raw meat or poultry and before they touch another food. Put cooked meat on a clean platter, rather back on one that held the raw meat.

*Chill:* Refrigerate leftovers promptly. Bacteria can grow quickly at room temperature, so refrigerate leftover foods if they are not going to be eaten within 4 hours. Large volumes of food will cool more quickly if they are divided into several shallow containers for refrigeration.

*Clean:* Wash produce. Rinse fresh fruits and vegetables in running tap water to remove visible dirt and grime. Remove and discard the outermost leaves of a head of lettuce or cabbage. Because bacteria can grow well on the cut surface of fruit or vegetable, be careful not to contaminate these foods while slicing them up on the cutting board, and avoid leaving cut produce at room temperature for many hours. As a home cook, don't be a source of foodborne illness yourself. Wash your hands with soap and water before preparing food. Avoid preparing food for others if you yourself have a diarrheal illness. Changing a baby's diaper while preparing food is a bad idea that can easily spread illness.

## Report

Report suspected foodborne illnesses to your local health department. The local public health department is an important part of the food safety system. Often calls from concerned citizens are how outbreaks are first detected. If a public health official contacts you to find our more about an illness you had, your cooperation is important. In public health investigations, it can be as important to talk to healthy people as to ill people. Your cooperation may be needed even if you are not ill.

## ARE SOME PEOPLE MORE LIKELY TO CONTRACT A FOODBORNE ILLNESS? IF SO, ARE THERE SPECIAL PRECAUTIONS THEY SHOULD TAKE?

Some persons at particularly high risk should take more precautions:

Pregnant women, the elderly, and those with weakened immune systems are at higher risk for severe infections such as *Listeria* and should be particularly careful not to consume undercooked animal products.

They should avoid soft French-style cheeses, pates, uncooked hot dogs, and sliced deli meats, which have been sources of *Listeria* infections. Persons at high risk should also avoid alfalfa sprouts and unpasteurized juices.

A bottle-fed infant is at most risk for severe infections with salmonella or other bacteria that can grow in a bottle of warm formula if it is left at room temperature for many hours. Particular care is needed to be sure the baby's bottle is cleaned and disinfected and that leftover milk formula or juice is not held in the bottle for many hours.

Persons with liver disease are susceptible to infections with a rare but dangerous microbe called *Vibrio vulnificus*, found in oysters. They should avoid eating raw oysters.

## WHAT CAN CONSUMERS DO WHEN THEY EAT IN RESTAURANTS?

You can protect yourself first by choosing which restaurant to patronize. Restaurants are inspected by the local health department to make sure they are clean and have adequate kitchen facilities. Find out how restaurants did on their most recent inspections, and use that score to help guide your choice. While this is not true in many jurisdictions, the latest Inspector's Report may be posted in the restaurant. Some restaurants have specifically trained their staff in principles of food safety. This is also good to know in deciding which restaurant to patronize.

You can also protect yourself from foodborne disease when ordering specific foods, just as you would at home. When ordering a hamburger, ask for it to be cooked to a temperature of 160 degrees F., and send it back if it is still pink in the middle. Before you order something that is made with many eggs pooled together, such as scrambled eggs, omelets, or French toast, ask the waiter whether it was made with pasteurized egg, and choose something else if it was not.

## HOW CAN FOOD BE MADE SAFER IN THE FIRST PLACE?

There is only so much the consumer can do. Making food safe in the first place is a major effort, involving the farm and fishery, the production plant or factory, and many other points from the farm to the table. Many different groups in public health, industry, regulatory agencies, and academia have roles to play in making the food supply less contaminated.

Consumers can promote general food safety with their dollars, by purchasing foods that have been processed for safety. For example, milk pasteurization was a major advance in food safety that was developed 100 years ago. Buying pasteurized milk rather than raw unpasteurized milk still prevents an enormous number of foodborne diseases every day. Now juice pasteurization is a recent important step forward that prevents *E. coli O157:H7* infections, *salmonella,* and many other diseases. Consumers can look for and buy pasteurized fruit juices and ciders.

In the future, meat and other foods will be available that has been treated for safety with irradiation. These new technologies are likely to be as important a step forward as the pasteurization of milk.

Foodborne diseases are largely preventable, though there is no simple one-step prevention measure like a vaccine. Instead, measures are needed to prevent or limit contamination all the way from farm to table.

A variety of good agricultural and manufacturing practices can reduce the spread of microbes among animals and prevent the contamination of foods. Careful review of the whole food production process can identify the principal hazards, and the control points where contamination can be prevented, limited, or eliminated. A formal method for evaluating the control of risk in foods exists is called the Hazard Analysis Critical Control Point, or HACCP system that is mentioned in the Introduction.

Early in the century, large botulism outbreaks occurred when canned foods were cooked insufficiently to kill the botulism spores. After research was done to find out exactly how much heat was needed to kill the spores, the canning industry and the government regulators went to great lengths to be sure every can was sufficiently cooked. As a result, botulism related to commercial canned foods has disappeared in this country.

Similarly, the introduction of careful pasteurization of milk eliminated a large number of milk-borne diseases. This occurred after sanitation in dairies had already reached a high level.

In the future, other foods can be made much safer by new pasteurizing technologies, such as in-shell pasteurization of eggs, and irradiation of ground beef. Just as with milk, these new technologies should be implemented in addition to good sanitation, not as a replacement for it.

So, in the end, it is up to the consumer to demand a safe food supply; up to industry to produce it; up to researchers to develop better ways of doing so; and up to government to see that it happens, to make sure it works and to identify problems still in need of solutions.

## WHAT IS CDC DOING TO CONTROL AND PREVENT FOODBORNE DISEASE?

- The Centers for Disease Control and Prevention (CDC) is part of the U. S. Public Health Service, with a mission to use the best scientific information to monitor, investigate, control, and prevent public health problems. Using the tools of epidemiology and laboratory science, CDC provides scientific assessment of public health threats. CDC works closely with state health departments to monitor the frequency of specific diseases and conducts national surveillance for them.

- CDC provides expert epidemiologic and microbiologic consultation to health departments and other federal agencies on a variety of public health issues, including foodborne disease, and it stations epidemiologists in state health departments to help with the surveillance and investigation of many problems.

- CDC can also send a team into the field to conduct emergency field investigations of large or unusual outbreaks, in collaboration with state public health officials. CDC researchers develop new methods for identifying, characterizing and fingerprinting the microbes that cause disease. We translate laboratory research into practical field methods that can be used by public health authorities in states and counties.

- CDC is not a regulatory agency. Government regulation of food safety is carried out by the Food and Drug Administration (FDA), the U.S. Department of Agriculture (USDA), the National Marine Fisheries Service, and other regulatory agencies.

- CDC maintains regular contact with the regulatory agencies. When new public health threats appear, CDC learns what they are and how they can be controlled through rapid scientific field and laboratory investigation. CDC shares the results of these investigations with the states, with the regulatory federal agencies and with the industries themselves. Although CDC does not regulate the safety of food, CDC assesses the effectiveness of current prevention efforts and provides independent scientific assessment of what the problems are, how they can be controlled, and of where there are gaps in the knowledge of the CDC staff.

## WHAT ARE SOME UNSOLVED PROBLEMS IN FOODBORNE DISEASE?

As new foodborne problems emerge, several questions need to be answered before the problem can be successfully controlled. It takes careful scientific observation and research to answer these questions.

Some pressing unanswered questions include:

How do the foodborne pathogens spread among the animals themselves, and how can this be prevented?

This includes *E. coli O157:H7* among cattle, *Salmonella enteritis* among egg-laying hens, and *campylobacter* in broiler chickens.

If it were possible to prevent the animals from becoming infected in the first place, there would not be as much illness in the humans who eat them.

## WHAT IS THE MICROBIAL CAUSE OF OUTBREAKS IN WHICH NO PATHOGEN CAN BE IDENTIFIED BY CURRENT METHODS?

This is true for over half of the reported foodborne outbreaks. Will wider application of existing experimental diagnostic methods help, or are these outbreaks caused by pathogens we simply do not yet know how to identify?

What would be the impact of basic food safety education of restaurant workers on the risk of foodborne disease among restaurant patrons?

How can the food and water that animals consume be made safer?

How can we dispose of animal manure usefully, without threatening the food supply and the environment?

How can basic food safety principles be most effectively taught to school children?

How can we be sure food safety standards in other countries are as good as those in the United States? As we import more of our fresh foods from other countries, we need to be confident that they are produced with the same level of safety as food in the United States.

What control strategies in the slaughter plant will reduce the contamination of poultry meat with *campylobacter*?

How can irradiation pasteurization of certain high risk foods, such as ground beef, be used most effectively?

How do raspberries in Central America get contaminated with *cyclospora* in the first place? Does this parasite have an animal reservoir?

How can alfalfa sprouts and other raw sprouts be produced safely? Sprouts are unique among foods in that the conditions for sprouting are also perfect for bacterial growth, and they are not cooked after that.

# Careers Available in Food Safety

According to *The Food Safety Information Handbook* by Cynthia A. Roberts, Oryx Press, many trade associations and professional societies offer scholarship, internship, or fellowship opportunities. If *Food-Safe Kitchens* has made you more aware of this important subject, and has given you a passion to seek a career in the culinary field, here, from Roberts' valuable book, is a list to call for more information:

American Culinary Federation, Inc.
St. Augustine, FL
800-624-9458

offers scholarships
www.acschefs.org

American Dietetic Association (ADA)
Chicago, IL
800-877-1600

offers scholarships
www.eatright.org

American Institute of Baking (AIB)
Manhattan, KS
(785) 537-4750 x179

offers scholarships
www.aibonline.org

American School Food Service Association (ASFSA)
Alexandria, VA
(703) 739-3900

offers scholarships, internships—
call and info will be mailed to you
www.asfsa.org

American Society for Healthcare
 Food Service Administrators (ASHFSA)
Chicago, IL
(312) 422- 3870

www.ashfsa.org

Centers for Disease Control and Prevention (CDC)      www.cdc.gov
Atlanta, GA
(770) 488-3257

Institute of Food Technologists (IFT)      www.ift.org
Chicago, IL
(312)-782-8424

International Association      www.iacpfoundation.org
 of Culinary Professionals (IACP)
Louisville, KY
(502) 581-9786

National Association of College      www.nacufs.org
 and University Food Services (NACUFS)
E. Lansing, MI
(517) 332-2494

National Environmental Health Association (NEHA)      ask for Megan Thompson
Denver, CO
(303) 756-9090


Write for a scholarship application and information.


The Asparagus Club Scholarship
Send request to: Scholarship Program Administrators, Inc.
P.O. Box 23737
Nashville, TN 27202-3737

National Meat Association (NMA)      ask for Jenny for info
Oakland, CA
(510) 763-1533

National Restaurant Association Educational Foundation      www.nra.org
Chicago, IL
800 765-2122 x733

# Index

## A

allergy, food. See food allergy
anaphylaxis, 53, 64
asthma, 63, 64
atopic dermatitis, 63

## B

baby food regulations, 13
bacteria
    foodborne illnesses caused by, 35t,
      36t, 37t, 38t
    in moist foods, 81
    refrigeration as prevention, 81
beef/pork/lamb
    color as unreliable indicator of done-
      ness, 42
    internal temperature, 26, 29, 42, 49t
    purchasing, what to look for when,
      11

roasts, 88
underdone, 29
botulism, 124

## C

calicivirus, 117
campylobacter, 116–117
canned goods, dented, 13
careers in food safety, 128–129
Centers for Disease Control and
    Prevention, 125–126
Chantos, Robert J., 25, 31, 79
cheeses, soft, 74, 123
chicken/poultry
    internal temperature, 26, 42,
      49t
    purchasing, what to look for when,
      11–12
    Thanksgiving turkey safety, 83
    underdone, 29

children, food safety issues/training, 70–71
cider, unpasteurized, 82
cleaning vs. sanitization, 8
cleanliness, handwashing. (see hand-washing)
Clostridium botulinum, 117
coconut allergy, 57
cold chain, 9, 14
cold foods. See also refrigerator
    keeping cold, 28, 29, 90
    Two-Hour Rule, 28, 90
Cooperative Extension, 111t, 112t, 113t, 114t, 115t
cross-contamination
    counters, sanitizing, 28
    definition, 27
    entertaining at home, when, 81. (see also entertaining)
    examples, 27
    from playground, 4
    school lunch preparations, during, 98–99
    separating foods, 28
cutting boards, 29

**D**

dashboard dining. See traveling, dining while
deli case warm foods, 13
Dominick, Tom, xii
Donley, Nancy, 103
dough, raw, 81
Doyle, Dr. Michael P., xiii
dry foods, insect infestation, 12. See also insects
dry ice, 105

**E**

Easter eggs. See under eggs
eating out, food safety issues, 75

E. Coli, 117, 118, 126
    coleslaw case, 17
    Lane County case, 6–7
eggnog, 88
eggs
    allergy to, 55
    Easter safety, 91–92
    FAAN information, 60
    internal temperature, 26, 49t
    refrigerating, 81
    uncracked, use only, 13
Eight Food–Safe Steps, 3–31
entertaining
    buffet issues, 80
    double dipping of foods, 80
    finger foods, 80
    fondue pots, 81
    food gifts, 87–88
    food safety issues, 79
    foodborne infections linked to, 80
    ice, 80
    plates, fresh, for refills/seconds, 81
    Thanksgiving food safety, 83–86
expiration dates, 8, 10–11

**F**

First In First Out, 18
fish. See seafood
flu
    shot, with egg allergy, 55
    vs. foodborne illness, 39
fondue pots, 81
food allergy
    definition, 53
    egg, 55
    fish/shellfish, 57, 58
    gastrointestinal symptoms of, 63
    milk. (see milk allergy)
    most common types of, 53–54, 63
    outgrowing, 56
    peanut, 56
    soy, 58–59

tree nut, 56–57
vs. food intolerance, 59–60, 63–64
vs. foodborne illness, 62
wheat, 59
Food Education Safety Staff, xii
food gifts, 87–88
food intolerance, 59–60, 63–64, 103
food thermometer. See thermometer,
    food
food transport, 89–90
food, perishable. (see perishable food)
foodborne illnesses
    causes, 116
    chart of, 35t, 36t, 37t, 38t
    common, most, 116–118
    contamination of food by, 120, 121
    coping with, 103
    discoveries, recent, 118
    doctor, when to see, 118
    foods most often associated with,
        121, 122
    health department tracking, 118,
        119
    high-risk individuals, 123
    outbreaks, 119, 120
    prevalence/incidences, 118
    protection against, 122–123
    restaurant safety, 123–124
    spread of, 117
    symptoms, 39
    vs. food allergy, 62
Frantz, Todd, xii, 4
Fraser, Angela, 31
freezer
    dates/times for various products, 20t,
        21t, 22t
frozen foods, case temperatures, 12–13
fruits/vegetables. See also produce; veg-
    etables, frozen
    as foodborne illness carriers, 124
    brush, scrubbing with, 18
    categories of refrigeration, 16, 17
    ethylene gas in, 23, 24

freshness, 12
ripening, 19, 22
storing in refrigerator, 18
washing, how to, 18
washing, when to, 17, 18

**G**

germs, 35t, 36t, 37t, 38t
glass jar seals, 12
grapefruit see extract, 19
grocery shopping. See shopping,
    grocery

**H**

haepatitis A, 103
ham
    canned, 19
    internal temperature, 49t
handwashing
    booklet, free, on, 6
    frequency/when to, 4
    importance, 4–5
    nailbrush use, 3, 5
    posters, 5
    technique, 3
    traveling, when, 97
    unpacking groceries, when, 16
hives, 63
holiday food preparation, 83–92
Hutchins, John-Paul, 4–5
hygiene. See also cross-contamination;
    sanitization
    handwashing. (see handwashing)
    pets in the home, 75

**I**

ice cream, purchasing, 13
ice, safety issues, 80
immune-compromised persons, food
    safety issues for, 67–69

insects, 107, 108
intolerance, food. See food intolerance

## J

juices, raw, 65–66, 74

## K

kitchen, sanitization. See sanitization,
    kitchen

## L

lamb. See beef/pork/lamb
lead poisoning, 107
learn more about food safety,
    116–127
leftovers, 31, 32, 82, 88, 90
Lerman, Dion, xii
Linzy, Steve, xii, 4, 8
listeria, 68
Ludwig, David, xii, 31, 64

## M

Mc Peak, Holly, xiii, 41
Mc Swane, David, PhD, xii
meat. See beef/pork/lamb
Meer, Ralph, PhD, xiii, 96
milk allergy
    baking if one has, 54
    cow vs. goat milk, 54
    FAAN information, 60
    managing, 54
    milk proteins, 55
mise en place, 30
Misner, Scottie, PhD, 96
MMR vaccine, with egg allergy, 55

## N

Norton, L. Charnette, xiii

Norwalk virus, 116
nutmeg allergy, 57

## O

O'Neil, Carolyn, 93
odors of foods, 22, 23

## P

pack date, 11
parasites, foodborne illnesses caused by,
    37t
parchment paper, use when cooking, 27
pasteurization
    cider, 82
    importance, 13
    reduction of illnesses associated
        with, 125
    vs. raw juices, 65, 74
peanut allergy, 56, 60
perishable food
    cooler use, in trunk of car when
        shopping, 9
    handling safely, 8–9
    room temperature, limits on how
        long kept at, 13, 74
    transporting, 94
pets, hygiene care with, 75
picnicking
    cold foods, 96
    food transport, 94
    perishables, 96
    safety issues, 96
poisons, 107
pork. See beef/pork/lamb
potluck meals, 89–90
poultry. See chicken/poultry
Powitz, Robert, PhD, xiii, 16, 19,
    103
pregnant women, food safety issues for,
    67–69, 123
produce. See also fruits/vegetables